PRACTICAL PARENTING

ALSO BY MONTEL WILLIAMS

● ●

Life Lessons and Reflections
Mountain, Get Out of My Way!

ALSO BY JEFFREY GARDÈRE, PH.D.

● ●

Smart Parenting for African Americans

PRACTICAL PARENTING

MONTEL WILLIAMS
AND JEFFREY GARDÈRE, PH.D.

MOUNTAIN
MOVERS
PRESS

an imprint of Hay House, Inc.
Carlsbad, California • Sydney, Australia

Published and distributed in the United States by:
Mountain Movers Press, an imprint of Hay House, Inc., P.O. Box 5100, Carlsbad, CA 92018-5100 • (800) 654- 5126 • (800) 650-5115 (fax) www.hayhouse.com

Editorial supervision: Jill Kramer • *Design:* Jenny Richards

Library of Congress Cataloging-in-Publication Data

Williams, Montel.
    Practical parenting / Montel Williams and Jeffrey Gardere.
        p.   cm.
    Includes bibliographical references.
    ISBN 1-58825-000-8 (hc.)
        1. Parenting. I. Gardere, Jeffrey Roger. II. Title.

HQ755.8 .W5344 2000
649'.1--dc21   00-060928

ISBN 1-58825-000-8

03 02 01 00   4 3 2 1
1st printing, September 2000

Printed in the United States of America

CONTENTS

● ●

Acknowledgments

●●●●●●●●●●●●●●●●●●●●●●●●●●●●●●

I would like to thank the following people for making this book possible: Melanie McLaughlin, my manager; and Angela Lee, president of Mountain Movers Press, who nurtured and parented this book from its conception; Daniel Paisner, who harnessed my voice and energy—a daunting task for any one person; Reid Tracy and Daniel Levin of Hay House, Inc., for their nudges, deadlines, and unwavering support—without them, this would just be a parenting manuscript.

To Ashley, Maressa, Montel II, and Wynter-Grace—although my parenting of you is practical, my love for you is not—it is unquestionable, unreserved, and an inimitable reminder of all that is good in the world. Parenting you is my most satisfying, most challenging, and most humbling of tasks, and I hope one day that it will be my greatest accomplishment.

— Montel Williams

I would like to thank Angela Lee and Melanie McLaughlin, the fearless leaders of LETNOM, for dropping the bug in Montel's ear that Dr. Jeff should be the shrink involved in this parenting project. Also, Nancy Goldman for her continued kindness in including me in Montel's newsletters. Daniel Paisner has given me a newfound respect for "professional" writers. My dear sister, Barbara, whose encouragement means even more to me now that she is gone. My wife, Deyanira, who has been my classmate in the school of life. And, of course, my children, Q'vanaa and Puma, who have allowed me to gain the personal experience of being a parenting expert.

— Jeffrey Gardère, Ph.D.

⦙⦙CHAPTER⦙⦙
ONE

PRACTICAL PRE-PARENTING

The two of us approach the complicated issue of parenting from diverse backgrounds that somehow converged on the set of the TV program *Montel*. It might seem like an improbable place for a partnership such as this one to take root, but it's turned out to be the most natural thing in the world. Fate . . . karma . . . a collision waiting to happen . . . and it happened, predictably, on television.

Jeff: Montel, of course, is the host of one of the longest-running and most popular talk shows on syndicated television, where he regularly interviews parents and families, and counsels them on a variety of issues.

Montel: Jeff, a leading family therapist, talk-radio personality, and founder of Rainbow Psychological Services in New York City, was booked on my show as an expert on family matters. Between segments, we struck up an easy friendship that focused on our deep commitment to helping people help themselves.

We are, as we've come to realize in the long hours spent working on this project, cut from the same cloth. Our goals are a lot alike, even though our training and our methods are completely different—and our careers, on paper, are as far apart as could be. One of us is by-the-book, and the other is on-the-fly.

Montel: As a clinical psychologist with a Ph.D. from George Washington University, Jeff approaches his work from an academic perspective, embracing accepted diagnostic models and recognized therapeutic techniques.

Jeff: Montel, a Naval intelligence officer-turned motivational-speaker-turned family-centric television personality, has visited with thousands of families in crisis on his program, where he deploys his unique and focused brand of in-your-face, on-the-air therapy to help patch the trouble spots in the lives of his guests.

For both of us, the fractured state of the American family and the troubled condition of America's children are what drive us in our work. What we've seen, over and over, are parents who are ill-equipped for the tough task of helping their kids thrive in a difficult world. Ill-equipped, ill-advised, ill-prepared—you name it—so what we mean to do here is attempt to cure at least some of those ills.

The easy joke, lately, has been that newborn children should come with a set of instructions when they leave the pediatric ward if parents ever hope to learn how to operate them. Obviously, a book on parenting, at best, can never be more than a book on . . . parenting. It's just a tool—little more than that hoped-for set of instructions that for some reason never materializes. It can never replace the real work that families must do to create smart, practical, nurturing environments in which our children can grow to become smart, practical, nurturing adults. However, for many of us, it can be a place to start, and a valuable point of reference.

So, we've put our heads together to offer up some practical observations and straight-talking commentary, in the hopes that *our* take might spur you, our readers, to scratch your own heads a little bit and discover a couple things you didn't know. Or, a couple things you *did* know back there in a dusty little corner of your brains, but haven't thought about, or at least, not precisely in this way. This is a book that might jump-start parents toward the real work you must do on yourselves before you can even begin to think about the real work that lies ahead. We don't purport to be the end-all in parenting books. No way. You see, this book is not an *end* so much as it is a *beginning*—a starting point.

We fully expect you (new and veteran parents, as well as those *thinking* about being parents someday) to read everything you can get your hands on, try every piece of homespun advice you hear, and learn from your own mistakes—just as we, as parents, have done—and continue to do. We just want to be in the mix, a part of the chorus, because we come at this thing from an extraordinary pair of front-row seats. Personally. Professionally. *Practically.* It's a chance for us to address forward-thinking parents on a bunch of things that have been keeping us up nights. Some things we've been thinking about. Some things we think you should be thinking about, too.

So let's get busy. . . .

Parenting in Public

Have you ever found yourself in a public place—a movie theater, a mall, or maybe a park—and caught yourself looking at how different sets of parents and children go through the motions of being a family? It's an amazing cultural phenomenon, and yet what's also amazing is how few of us think to carefully observe the parenting styles around us before deciding to start a family ourselves. Sure, we've always got our own parents to use as models, but that's a limited example. Why go with one or two frames of reference when there's a whole inventory out there waiting to be discovered?

Looking back, we sometimes find ourselves wishing that someone had sent *us* to DisneyWorld, or to the sidelines of a Little League game, or to a school play in a strange town—*before* we ever thought of having kids. These places are like perfect Petri dishes for brewing family issues, but it's as if they exist in a vacuum for all the good they do for the prospective parent.

Think about it. Who goes to a family vacation resort without children? Who attends opening night of the movie *Chicken Run* unescorted by at least one G-rated kid? Who shops at Toys 'R' Us? Prospective parents should definitely shake up their universe a little bit, and check some of these places out before trying on their new roles.

Start eye-balling people, and make some notes to yourself on how parents interact with their kids. Try to find the good, the bad, and the ugly—because it's all out there on constant display. Pay special attention to families in stressful situations: through the car windows in a bumper-to-bumper traffic jam, standing in line for the thrill-ride-of-the-moment at the local amusement park, or at the local hair-cutting salon.

Take the pieces you like, toss out the pieces you don't, and at the other end, you'll have a better picture of the kind of parent you'd like to be—or, at least, the kind of *public* parent you'd like to be. Now, this takes us to an essential point: A lot of folks, we've found, have different notions of acceptable ways to act in the privacy of their homes, versus how they act out in public.

One of the things we see a lot, for example, is the way certain parents berate their children in public places. Actually, *berate* is probably too civilized a word for what these people do to their kids. They yell. They humiliate. They grab their kids' little arms like they're made of rubber. They go off the deep end. It's the kind of tragedy that gets played out on a daily basis, in every community, over and over and over. We hate to generalize, but usually you'll see this type of behavior in transparently undereducated, low-income families. Still, despite its predominance in our poorer, inner-city communities, this kind of public scolding from parent to child is *everywhere*. It knows no economic or social class. It's not black or white or brown. It's the way certain types of people respond when they're overwhelmed and overmatched, and if you're going to pattern yourself along the lines of what you see on the street, this is one pattern of behavior you would do well to avoid.

If you're one of these folks we've just described, how can you yell at your child like that in front of other people? Not only is it embarrassing and disruptive, but it also places you at the bottom of this particular food chain. It's low-class. It's demeaning. It's so far beneath who you are and who you're aiming to be that it's barely worth the paragraph or two we've taken to set it out on these pages.

And as long as we're on this subject, know this: Volume doesn't automatically equate to understanding. In fact, your kid will be more likely to tune out your screaming and barking than listen to what you have to say, even if what you have to say is quite reasonable. There's usually enough going on in the conversation without mortifying the kid in the bargain.

The suggestion here is not to go looking for negative examples of parental behavior, but to take in the whole spectrum. Don't judge. Go out there in the world you're inhabiting and learn how it is from all sides. It's a picture you tend not to see until you're right in it, so seek it out and see what you can see. You'll find wonderfully nurturing parents, with all kinds of creative energy; and you'll find bored, complacent parents who seem to want to be anywhere else than with their kids. You'll find single mothers, somehow managing to answer questions from co-workers on their cell phones, while at the same time cleaning a scraped knee after their kid falls off the jungle gym. You'll see divorced, visitation-rights dads, struggling to make conversation with their adolescent daughters over ice cream. You'll see kids calling all the shots, while their parents seem to be there just to pay for each new whim.

And then there are the wonderful variations on this baseline theme. We saw one young mother just the other day at the grocery store, wheeling her newborn baby in a canopied stroller. Man, was that child decked out! The mother had this tiny little boy dressed just so, with one of those little halo pillows around his neck to keep him from moving from side to side. His legs were supported by another tiny cushion. All around, you could just see the effort this woman had made for this child. The kid couldn't have been more than a couple weeks old, and it's possible that this was one of his first public outings and the mother was still overdoing things, but her attentiveness went beyond the clothing and accessories. Every few steps, she would kind of lean in from behind the stroller to check on the kid, because the canopy was set up in such a way that the child was blocked from her view when she pushed the stroller from behind. She was fussing with the child, making sure he was okay and comfortable and breathing properly, and whatever else it is that new mothers check, and what was clear was that this was a woman who was absolutely ready to be a parent. She recognized the importance of the task—seemed to relish it, actually—and took the responsibility seriously.

Contrast that with another woman we saw a couple days later who dragged her toddler around like she was a little rag doll. The kid's face was a chocolate mess, her hair was wild and unkempt, her clothes were in need of a wash and iron, and from the way her mother pulled her around on her errands, the child might have been a piece of carry-on luggage. The distinction here was not a matter of culture or station. Both mothers appeared to have enough money to dress their children in any way they chose, and both were shopping in high-end stores. No, the differences had to do with style and personality.

It takes all kinds, and it's up to you, in this pre-parenting stage of your life, to reflect on what kind of parent you'd like to be. We've never actually tried the DisneyWorld observation strategy ourselves without our own kids in tow, but we can't think of a broader canvas for your parental styling tour. It's all there, in one kingdom or another—in every shape, form, and dynamic you can imagine. (It even takes some unimaginable forms, as well!) If you can't swing the time or the finances for a Disney-type vacation, a kids' matinee will do. The point here is to get you moving about and looking at the world in a new way—before it's too late.

A Parenting Plan

Naturally, all this reflection will most likely get tossed out the door once your child arrives and you start winging it from one activity to the next, but you've got to have a plan, a model, a map. You can stray from the map, but it would be foolish to start off on such a significant journey without at least some type of blueprint, right? For many of us, that map is experience-based. The trouble is, we're basing that map on other people's experiences—usually on our parents'. We've got a good idea of what we *don't* want to do, based on what they did wrong, as well as what we hope to *excel* at, based on what they did right. And, if we're planning a traditional, two-parent household, we've got the legacy of our partner's parents to deal with, too.

We've all heard friends say things such as, "Oh, I can't believe it. I sound so much like my mother!" Or, "I just waved my father's finger at my child!" Usually, the implication is that such actions are a negative thing, that they represent a new low in parenting history, whereas the truth is that we've simply fallen back on what we know. And what we know isn't always as terrible as we think. Many of us have vowed not to repeat the mistakes of our parents, even though some of those mistakes are unavoidable. And some of those mistakes don't go much beyond the category of errors in judgment. As a child, you want your parent to be easygoing, to almost be like an older sibling; but as a parent, you recognize that strong parenting sometimes requires you to be hard, to be more disciplinarian than friend.

Go ahead—make a list of your mother and father's parenting techniques. Get your partner to make a similar list. Consider what you liked and what you disliked about the way you were raised. Consider, too, what you objected to as a child but understand and accept now from an adult perspective. And finally, consider the missteps your parents took that you hope to never repeat. When you've completed the list, hang it on the wall, in a prominent place, as a constant reminder of the only working blueprint you'll ever have for the role you're about to take on. One of the great side benefits of this exercise is the chance it might afford you to discuss some of these hits and misses with your folks when they stop by for a visit, in order to get their take on things. You might find that what you once regarded as horrific is backed up by a perfectly sensible explanation, and that what you once celebrated and cherished was backed into as a happy accident. You never know. The important lesson here is that a great chunk of the job of the practical parent is played out by instinct, and sometimes those instincts can strike parent and child from two completely distinct perspectives.

Another list we tell prospective parents to make is one that details all the dreams they have for their unborn child or children. Here again, let's give it a shot. Make your wish list as extensive as you want. Do you want your children to go to college? Be in the space program? Play professional ball? Anchor the evening news? Do you want them to marry, have children, and live in a big ol' house on a big ol' piece of land? Think it through, and then set it down on paper. Notice, here, that we don't suggest you hang up this list for prominent display. Quite the opposite. In fact, once you make this list, we want you to crumple it up and throw it away. Because, when you break it down, this is *not* a list that parents should make on behalf of their children. It doesn't matter that a couple of blowhard psychobabbling authors suggested the idea. The practical parent should know better. How dare you dream for your children? How dare you put your wishes ahead of theirs?

Your children need to create their own dreams, not live through yours. It's okay to wish for something, or hope for the best, but we have to let our children determine their own paths, their own goals. When you start dreaming about what it is you want your children to accomplish, you start setting expectations for them to live the life that *you* might not have gotten the chance to live. You put a cap on what they might accomplish on their own.

Instead of dreaming for your children, encourage them to think for themselves, dream for themselves, do for themselves. Don't start pushing your agenda on them, because you'll wind up with kids who put too much weight on pleasing you and not nearly enough on pleasing themselves.

Some parents have a hard time separating what it is they want for themselves from what it is they want for their children. We know; we've been there.

Montel: Jeff, in fact, is still there, in this one particular dream. He's forever pushing his son, who's seven, to become a jazz musician. It's a gentle kind of pushing, but it's pushing just the same, even though, intellectually, Jeff realizes that what he's doing contradicts the advice he might give his patients. He'll play Coltrane until the apartment fairly pulses with musical genius, but his kid's just not interested—and yet it's a tough dream to let die. It was tough for Jeff when it died in him, the first time around, and tough all over again when Jeff realized that his son's gifts lay someplace else.

The thing is, with this parenting deal, it's not about *you*; it's about your child. All down the line, every step of the way, it's about your child. Even if the decision to have kids was once about *you*, in some way, it's soon enough about the *child. Just* about the child. That said, one of the first things you need to do before that kid arrives is clean house. We don't mean with a feather duster— although, frankly, that's one of the great ways a "nesting" pre-parent can prepare for the new arrival. We mean for you to get your *emotional* house in order. Your personal baggage. The *stuff* you've carried around with you since forever. What you need to do is separate the pieces that have to do with *you* from the pieces that have to do with your reasons for bringing a child into this world. There's baggage that your parents put on you, baggage that others put on you, and—most important—the baggage you put on yourself. Let's be honest, we've all got a matched set of personal baggage, and we need to leave it at the door before crossing the threshold into parenthood.

Remember, becoming a parent is not something that just *happens*. It's not a passive act. Sure, we understand that getting pregnant can sometimes just *happen*, but if you're old enough and mature enough to be fooling around, you're old enough and mature enough to think some of these other things through as well.

As you read through these pages and take our experiences into account, keep in mind our basic rules of practical parenting:

- *Be humble.* Admit that you can be wrong—and when the evidence mounts against you, be the first to admit to it.

- *Be patient.* Leave your ego behind when dealing with your kids, and give them time to come around to your way of seeing things; if your way makes sense, they'll get there eventually.

- *Be firm.* Be consistent, and stay on the same page as your partner. Kids have enough trouble dealing with authority, without wondering which sets of rules apply to which occasions.

- *Be flexible.* No, we're not contradicting ourselves here (at least we don't mean to!). Being a parent doesn't mean being the boss—it means being the leader—and if your kids seem to want to take things in a different direction, it's sometimes okay to help them take you there.

- *Be respectful.* Of your child. Of yourself. Of the relationship you share. Of the world around you.

- And this above all . . . *be practical.* Think a situation through before kicking into action. If it makes sense, then go for it. If it makes no sense at all, then go some other way.

As you move forward, always be mindful of the difference between *programming* your children for success, and *imposing* your notions of success *on them.* Invest in the foundation for your children, but let them handle the bricks and mortar. Let them develop their own beauty, their own confidence, their own dreams.

Grow them so that they might grow themselves—into full flower, on their own.

Mission Impossible

You've probably heard this one before . . .

Joseph, 37, and Helen, 36, desperately wanted to start a family. Married more than ten years, it seemed to them that they'd been trying forever. They'd been to dozens of fertility specialists and clinics, and had pretty much exhausted their savings trying to figure out what the problem was—if there even was a problem. As far as they were able to determine, there was nothing physically wrong with either of them. Joseph's sperm count was fine; Helen's ovaries were producing healthy eggs. Their doctors kept telling them to just keep trying. And they did.

Eventually, all that trying took its toll, though. It sapped their marriage of any sense of romance. Their lovemaking became an on-demand ritual, intended for reproduction purposes only, rather than as an act of love and intimacy. Separately, neither one of them could recall an intimate encounter that didn't have to do with getting pregnant. All of their emotional energies were bound up in this endless effort to conceive, to the point that Joseph and Helen gradually lost sight of what had brought them together as a couple in the first place. Not only that, but they lost sight of the fact that parenthood was not just about making a baby physically, but also creating an environment to support and guide that baby emotionally.

Finally, when Helen did become pregnant, the news was double-edged. Yes, they still wanted a child. Yes, outwardly, they were thrilled. But it was also true that the news made them realize that they had damaged each other so badly in pursuit of this pregnancy that they weren't sure they were ready to become parents. They were emotionally spent, and the gift of life now appeared to be a burden, or even a curse!

And so, they sought help, and when they came to Jeff's office, the goal was emotional stability. Joseph and Helen set about reestablishing their priorities and rebuilding the emotional connection they had once shared. They found ways to inject intimacy into the equation. They took a vacation. The couple realized that in order to prepare for the baby's arrival, they needed to forget about the baby—for a while, anyway. They needed to think of themselves, and each other, before they could think about the baby on the way. They needed to unpack some of that emotional baggage we talked about earlier in order to become emotionally ready to be loving and diligent parents and partners.

Basically, they had to reach back over ten years to reclaim their relationship, and then rebuild that relation-

ship to the point that they were really ready to become parents. It was where they stood ten years ago when they first set out to become pregnant, but after so much time, the ground underfoot had become unstable. The fact that this couple managed to do so much productive, 11th-hour work on their marriage is testimony to the love they shared, and the commitment they felt to the family they hoped to become.

Now, here's where the story gets wonderfully familiar. Not long after the birth of their daughter, a healthy girl named Emma, Joseph and Helen effortlessly conceived their second child. They weren't even thinking about it. They didn't dare dream that such a thing was possible, yet there it was.

Once they started sharing their story with friends, they discovered that they weren't alone. There was a whole army of parents out there, they realized, who'd struggled through a difficult first pregnancy and sailed through their second. There were even folks who succeeded only through in vitro *sterilization, and others who gave up on biological parenting and sought adoption alternatives—only to conceive naturally, without a thought. There's even research to support this phenomenon. The numbers suggest that conception is as much an emotional act as a physical one. If you're not ready to become a parent—truly ready— then your body will look for a way to tell you.*

And, if you're like Joseph and Helen, you'll find a way to listen.

❖ ❖ ❖

···CHAPTER···
TWO

THE PRACTICAL BUILDING BLOCK

Self-esteem. To our way of thinking, it's at the core of every healthy relationship. Parent-child. Husband-wife. Brother-sister. Friend-friend. It's basic. It even holds the key to the pride we take in ourselves. Without it, we're done—better, we'll never get started! And yet it's amazing to us how many intelligent, well-meaning, *practical* people can't see their way to feeling good enough about themselves to allow them to interact in a positive, meaningful way with the folks around them.

What's also amazing is that we can't even find a good definition of the term in our dictionaries. Really, we've got a stack of 'em piled high on the desk in front of us as we write this—Webster's, Random House, New World—you name it—and there's not a single interpretation that gets close to what we're looking for.

In some, *self-esteem* is merely listed with a bunch of other words with the prefix *self*, right there with *self-satisfied* and *self-indulged*—which basically means that *self-esteem* needs a better agent. That better agent, for now, is *you*. You've taken that first proactive step toward building a solid, smart, practical relationship with your child. You've hauled your butt into the bookstore, or down to the library, or onto the World Wide Web, to get your hands on a book that might help you through some of the paces, and here you are. Ready. Open. Willing to listen to what a couple of guys with a mountain of parenting and related professional experiences have to say about what it takes to raise an emotionally healthy child in an increasingly confusing world.

It takes a lot, actually. More than we could hope to share in a whole series of books. More than we can ever know ourselves. But the gateway to each and every successful parent-child relationship we've encountered—in our own lives and in our careers—is self-esteem, a confidence and respect for oneself and one's abilities that runs deep enough to allow a person to confront and conquer every conceivable challenge (and some inconceivable ones, too).

Children with low self-esteem have the deck stacked all the way against them in almost every aspect of their lives. On the other hand, children with high self-esteem have the confidence to succeed in school and elsewhere because they *believe* they're intelligent. They participate in sports and the arts because they know they're talented. They make friends easily and carry themselves with pride among their peers because they've been taught to take pride in their appearance. They dare to dream and turn those dreams into reality because they *know* they can. They don't do hard drugs because they love and value themselves too highly to be self-destructive.

The Origination of Self-Esteem

But where does all that self-esteem originate? Well, it largely comes from you, the parents. It's not genetic. It's not preprogrammed into our children through the luck of biology. It's not nature. It's nurture, pure and simple. It's an untapped resource, waiting to be mined by resourceful parents. It comes from the way you love, regard, and speak to your children, who will learn to believe in themselves if you believe in them. It comes from the way you love, regard, and speak about yourself. It comes from *your* extra efforts to support and encourage your *child's* extra efforts—big ones, little ones, and all those in between. It comes from the way you carry yourself, the way you allow yourself to be treated, the way you treat others, the way you look at the world, and the way the world looks back at you. It's contagious, and in this case, it's something that you want your child to catch and never let go of.

One of the great failures in parenting literature, and in the advice doled out by so-called experts, is the assumption that the parent-child relationship begins at birth. That's crap. (Please forgive our straight talk, but we're in the habit of calling it like we see it, so get used to it.) The way we look at it, the real work begins long before you can even consider having a child. Or, at least that's where it *should* begin, because that's where it all starts. The real work is all about *you*. We are, all of us, works in progress, and the work we do on ourselves has everything to do with the work we'll be able to do with our children once they arrive.

There are all kinds of books on the marketplace telling expectant mothers what to eat when they're pregnant, how to exercise, and how to balance work and home, but no one's talking about getting our houses in order in an emotional sense. No one emphasizes our emotional preparedness for parenthood, and you can baby-proof your house and eat all the right foods until you're blue in the face, but you're not really ready to be a parent until you're *really ready to be a parent*. Let's face it, if we're not comfortable with who we are and the paths we've chosen, then how can we ever hope to bring children into the picture and instill them with a positive viewpoint? How can we help our kids find their way if we can't find the way ourselves?

We've all known people who haven't been at the best place in their lives when they became parents—in fact, some of us have *been* those people, or have been brought into this world by those people!—but when you break it down and consider the prospects in just these terms, it's easy to see how it's an unworkable model. Sure, there are exceptions to every rule, and we understand that a pregnancy can sometimes catch you by surprise, but why go against the odds? Why set yourself or your child down an unnecessarily hard road?

Think about children with low self-esteem. They lose the race every time because they never leave the starting gate. They don't have the equipment, or the foundation. They don't have the confidence, or the belief in their own abilities. They don't have the emotional tools. They feel stupid, incompetent, and unworthy. Why? Chances are it's because they become so used to hearing that they're too stupid, or too lazy, or too this, or too that. Quite often, they hear these things from their own parents, who perhaps are feeling a bit too stupid or lazy themselves. (Probably, they picked this up from their *own* parents, and pass it on like some backward-thinking inheritance.)

Over time, low self-esteem children internalize these comments to where they become a part of them. Doing well in school becomes impossible. Developing a winning personality—out of the question. Reaching for lofty goals—unthinkable. And interacting with their peers? Forget about it. This lack of self-esteem becomes the main ingredient in a life of fear, failure, and self-hate, and it flows in a very direct and fundamental way from the self-esteem of the parents.

Show us a slightly overweight mother who's embarrassed about her appearance, and we'll show you a daughter who's overly obsessed with her own dress size. Or try this: Behind every father who's beaten down by his boss at work, there's an underachieving son who can't seem to please his father. You get the idea.

The message is clear: Do the work you need to do on yourself *before* you think about starting a family. And if it's the case that getting pregnant wasn't exactly the kind of thing you had a chance to think through, get your act together as soon as possible. You wouldn't dream of practicing medicine without earning your degree, or building a house without learning a thing or two about construction. And yet parents jump into the gene pool without even thinking about how deep the water is, or how treacherous those waters can be. It's the most important job you'll ever undertake, so why not treat it as such going in? We're not talking about the feeding, burping, and bottom-wiping aspect of things, because anyone can figure out that end (so to speak). You might screw up, but you won't screw up too badly. (And, for what it's worth, we'll toss in our two cents on some of these particulars a bit later on in these pages.) We're talking about the hard stuff— the care and feeding of your child's emotions, and your ability to help that child navigate some pretty rough terrain.

You Are the Role Model

It may be more than you bargained for, but *you* are the most important person in your children's lives, and they will depend on you to impart good feelings and nurturing every minute of the day. With that dependence comes your responsibility to role-model for your kids what it takes to move about in a positive light. Show unconditional love and acceptance—at the same time, expecting it from those around you. Avoid denigration and humiliation in your interaction with your children, and in the way you allow yourself to be treated by others. It's one thing to become angry over something your kids have done and address that issue in a constructive manner. It's quite another thing to lose your temper and attack them for the same transgression. And it's something else entirely to let your children witness an attack on you in one of your adult relationships.

Remember, the things you say leave an indelible impression on your child's self-image. And so do the things left unsaid. The way you present yourself—from the way you dress, to the way you keep house . . . all counts for something. Take pride in your appearance, and your children will take pride in theirs. Command respect, and your children will learn respect for others. Rejoice in your accomplishments, and your children will rejoice in theirs.

Practical parenting sometimes means showering praise on your children for even the slightest achievements, because it's through these small steps that they'll be encouraged to leave bigger footprints in the future. Practical parenting means that even when you feel irritable and annoyed at your children for not knowing how to do something, you refrain from showing that irritation and making them feel incompetent. Show forgiveness and understanding, and encourage them to try again. Practical parenting means standing as your children's biggest cheerleaders, and offering up the kind of constant, unflinching support they'll need to take on life—and win. And, practical parenting often means shouldering your own disappointments and putting on a brave face for the sake of your kids.

So, we repeat: *Without self-esteem, you are nothing.* To sell the point, let's look at the most superficial levels. We know one young woman who positively radiated beauty as a little girl in elementary school. She wasn't a classic beauty by any means—her nose was slightly off-center, and her face was a little too angular for the rest of her body—but to her parents, and others who loved her, she was the most beautiful little girl to ever grace the planet. And, she *was*. She walked to school every day, and nobody could tell her she wasn't beautiful. That's how she was treated at home, and that's how she carried herself. There was no high-falutin' air about her, no sense of entitlement, but she was supremely confident in her appearance, even though her appearance, by all conventional standards, was somewhat flawed.

Well, jump ahead 30 years to her high school reunion, and guess what? She was the most stunning creature in the room. Hands down. All around her there were nose jobs and face-lifts and tummy tucks, and enough extra pounds to fill a meat-packing plant, but this woman carried the day. Why? She was infused with a glorious inner beauty. She liked herself, and the way she looked, and the way those good looks made her feel inside. And we have to think it all flowed down from the way her parents treated her as a child.

Now, we like to believe as parents that our child's physical appearance is the least of our concerns, but if we're completely honest about it, we'll admit that it's far easier to move about in our society as a good-looking person than a plain-looking one. Give any parent a choice about whether they want their child to turn heads or turn stomachs, and they'll choose the former. Surely there's a reason for this, one that runs beyond simple vanity. Like it or not, we live in a world where appearances count. They do. They don't count for *everything*, mind you, but they count for a lot, and if you have the tools to help your children feel good about their appearance, then you better start using them.

The principal tool, of course, is feeling good about your *own* appearance—accepting who you are and the body you've been given. Ectomorph, endomorph, mesomorph . . . it doesn't matter what shape or size you are, as long as you're healthy, you pay attention to what you eat, you try to exercise a little bit, and you present yourself to the world with pride. Do the best job you can with the raw materials you've been given. Remember that Billy Crystal character, Fernando, from *Saturday Night Live*? His tag line was, "It's better to look good than to feel good," and it always got a laugh, but underneath the laugh line was a basic truth, because a positive attitude about your appearance inevitably leads to a positive attitude about your health and emotional well-being.

If your child watches you get stepped on at work, or disrespected at the checkout line, or taken advantage of by your auto mechanic, it rubs off. Better believe it, *it rubs off*. If you're so ill at ease with your own body image that you refuse to wear a swimsuit at the beach, it rubs off. If you're a single parent and your child sees you take multiple sex partners, it rubs off. It doesn't matter if that child is three, six, or nine months old, it rubs off. It doesn't matter if that child is three, six, or nine *years* old. And as long as we're talking about it, did you know that new single-parent mothers run the highest risk of unwanted pregnancy of any other group of single women? The research shows that soon after the birth of their first child, their self-esteem is so low that many new mothers look for someone to fill the void they feel in their lives, and they frequently wind up pregnant again. Look at teenage pregnancies—you'll often see them come in twos, because sometimes it takes two giant mistakes for a young woman to get her act together in the self-esteem department.

It's Time to Get Busy

Think back to why you picked up this book in the first place. Maybe you heard us talking about parenting issues on television, or maybe you read about the book in a newspaper or magazine. Maybe a friend suggested that you check out what we have to say. The point is, you cracked these covers to find some help, to learn a little something you didn't know—about yourself, about your child, and about navigating this interesting new territory.

Chances are, if you happen to fall into the single-mother, teenage pregnancy category, you didn't even think about your self-esteem before you got pregnant. It wasn't an issue. There's a good chance that this wasn't any kind of planned event in your life. But now your baby's here, and that baby's sitting in the other room, and you've come to this chapter and it hits you: You don't feel too good about yourself. In fact, just to play out this single-parent theme, there are strong odds to suggest that the baby itself is the product of your own low self-esteem. And the fact that the father didn't stick around now that the baby's been born? That's a product of *his* low self-esteem. Check that: Any man who fathers a child, knows about it, and does not participate in any way, shape, or form in the rearing of that child, is someone with no self-esteem at all!

The bottom-line message here is this: The time to get busy on your own self-esteem is *before* you get pregnant. If the ship has sailed on that count, you should at least confront these issues before the baby arrives; and if it's too late for *that*, at least it's not too late to make some improvements. Parenting is too big a deal to let it sneak up on you, so start thinking these things through the moment that the pregnancy test turns pink or blue or whatever color it is that signals you're expecting.

The messages you need to keep in mind are:

- *You are the only person who defines you.* It begins with you. It ends with you. It doesn't matter what other people think or feel or say. It's all up to you. Go to the mirror and see for yourself.

- *Clear your mind, and clear your plate.* Spend some time on this, because it matters. Give yourself a thorough going-over; becoming your harshest critic and your most ardent supporter. Make a list of all the things you like about yourself, the things you're good at, the accomplishments you've made, and your unique achievements. Know that your list doesn't have to be 500 miles long, but make the list.

- *Make the effort.* Indeed, make the *extra* effort. Make another list of all the hurtful things that people have said to you over the years. "Your hair's too stringy." "Your butt's too big." "Your voice is too loud." "Your manner's too intrusive . . ." Include on this list all those times you've second-guessed yourself, or botched some task that you know you could have handled differently. Also include all the negative things you've caught yourself thinking about your appearance, your work ethic, or the ways you interact with others. Put this book down for a little while, and give this exercise your best shot, because at the other end of it you'll have some of the tools you'll need to help redefine yourself in a more positive light.

Okay? Now, take a look at what you've written. A long, hard look. Hopefully, the positive side of the ledger will be somewhat longer than the negative, but don't get all freaky on us if it's not. Simply cross any entry off the negative list that you can't do a damn thing about. Thin lips. Big feet. Whatever. To be fair, cross off the positive list any entry that didn't have a thing to do with you, such as winning the lottery or a killer smile. Once you've whittled both lists down some, you can attack all those negative entries. If it's in your power to fix it, then fix it. Immediately. If you can't fix it straightaway, at least get started on it. Do you tend to gossip? Promise yourself you'll quit, immediately. Do you spend money foolishly? Become a smarter shopper. Do you cut corners at work? Start doing a better job. Do you fall into relationships too easily because you don't like being alone? Become a little more discriminating in your dating habits. Are you fighting with your spouse in front of the children? If so, take it behind closed doors.

And so on . . .

At some point, when you trim the things you can't do anything about and the things you can, you'll be left with very little to beat yourself up about. You'll just be left with all of your positive accomplishments, and these will really be something. These are the things that should define you. Each individual accomplishment—and it doesn't matter if it's big or small—adds up to who you are. They're building blocks to establishing confidence. Each positive achievement helps you love yourself a little bit more, and to raise the bar a little bit on what you might achieve next. Even our unfinished business is worthy of praise. Falling two credits shy of a college degree doesn't mean that you've failed horribly; it just means that you stand wonderfully close to finally graduating. It's all a matter of perspective.

Most important, though, is the way each positive achievement puts you in a better position to reinforce the best efforts of your child, and to temper that reinforcement so that it rings true. Kids are smarter than we know. We can't keep saying, "Oh, Sally, that's the best picture I've ever seen!" and expect Sally to hear it after the fifth or sixth time. If your child draws a nice picture and you want to compliment her on it, it's okay to call it nice or wonderful or interesting. Put it on the fridge, but don't put it on a pedestal. Everything our children do doesn't have to be the best, and if we fall into the trap of overpraising, we'll throw our credibility right out the window and push our kids toward false expectations.

See yourself as you truly are—not as others see you, and not as you wish to be seen. One way to do this is to ask yourself some tough questions, and learn where your answers place you on the spectrum. We've all taken those silly pop-psychology quizzes that turn up in our monthly magazines, but they're rarely about anything this important. For some reason, "Rating Your Television Habits" doesn't seem to measure up in the broader scheme of things.

Put your face back in that mirror, and turn the tables on yourself.

Do you like yourself?

Are you generally happy?

Do you regard yourself in a positive light?

Is it important to you that others think of you in a positive way?

Is there anything about your appearance that you'd like to change?

Are you proud of what you've accomplished in your life?

If you'd like, throw in some tough, relevant questions of your own, and then grade yourself on a five-point scale—with the 5 representing an extreme positive answer, and the 1 representing an extreme negative. Know that there are no correct answers. Every answer is *your* answer, a reflection of how you see yourself and the choices you've made.

If you wind up with all 3's, it's usually a good indicator that you see yourself as a middle-of-the-road kind of person; you're neither here nor there, and probably a little too willing to let someone else push you in one direction or another. If you wind up with all 5's, then it's clear that your parents did a very good job of instilling a strong sense of self and purpose in you, even if it might seem a little too strong. If you tally all 1's, then clearly you didn't need this little exercise to realize that you walk around in a funk, that you sell yourself short, and that the world sometimes seems too big a place for you to cut your path through. A couple of 2's and 4's suggest moderation, and room for improvement, but the real red flag is the constant waffling in the middle of the scale. Those are the people who need to reassess and redefine who they are and what they hope to become. Those are the people who feel trapped in a pattern of negativity, the ones who are more likely to experiment with drugs, the individuals who hop from one bed to the next with hardly a thought, and those who can't seem to advance on the job.

Juxtapose your state of mind on your own with your responsibilities as a new parent, and *get to work*. A child on the way is your last and best opportunity to redeem yourself, to set right the pendulum, to turn your life around. This is your chance to grow, and if you don't take it, you consign your child to a life lived on that same middle ground. If you've struggled with it, then why the hell would you want that same struggle for your kid? You could have messed up a dozen relationships, but it's how you handle the one you're in when your child arrives that really counts. Maybe you were fired from your last three jobs, but it's the job you hold and keep that will define you as a responsible parent. Find a way to think of yourself as a confident person, a supportive person, and a compassionate person, and it won't matter what anyone else says about you.

What matters is how you see yourself, and how your child views your perception. It doesn't matter if you're on public assistance, or if you're so deep in debt that you can't see your way out.

As long as you meet each day with hope and pride, that's what your child will take away from the situation.

And another thing. Don't go running your mouth off in front of your kids, because they'll pick up on it. *"Oh, Jimmy's so smart, but he's got no appetite." "She's an angel, but she's got her Daddy's nose." "Yeah, I know he's a big kid, but how come he's not walking yet?"* Even if your children are too young to understand the words, they'll hear the sentiment behind them, the disappointment.

As parents, we need to always remember that we man (and woman) the front lines of our children's definition of themselves. Our impulses are the first they take in, often ahead of their own, so be extremely careful what you say and how you say it. Distribute praise evenly among all of your children, for all that they do. Learning to go to the bathroom. Holding a fork. Sitting up. Sleeping through the night. But don't go over the top. Every little accomplishment doesn't have to be the best in the world. Every pretty little girl doesn't have to be the prettiest little girl in the world.

Jeff: In fact, Montel faced this issue with his own daughter, Wynter-Grace, when she was just turning five, on pretty much a daily basis. Then, as now, this child moved about with the supreme confidence of a little girl who knows she's got it going on. And she does. But it had been drummed into her in such a way that there was no room in her thinking for another child to be held in the same regard.

"Daddy," she used to say in a sad voice, pointing to a pretty little girl in a shopping mall, "that little girl over there, she's not as pretty as me."

"Oh, but she is, Wynter-Grace," Montel would answer back, with the loving firmness it took him four kids to learn.

Even so, Wynter-Grace usually started to cry.

"Why are you crying, baby?" Montel would ask.

"Because you said she's as pretty as me," she would respond.

"But she is," Montel insisted. "I'm sorry, baby, but she is.

In her parents' eyes, maybe she's even prettier. You are beautiful to us, in our eyes. We say you're the most beautiful child on the planet because you're *our* beautiful child. You're *our* daughter. That little girl right there, she's someone else's daughter, and they love her just as much as Mommy and I love you."

It's a tough balancing act, we know, to give your children enough of the positive impulses they'll need without going over the top a little bit, but it's a whole lot easier if it comes from a positive place. More natural. Less forced.

So get to work. If you don't like what you see staring back at you in the mirror, it doesn't mean you can't be an effective, practical parent. It just means that you have to change the picture a little bit before moving forward.

"It's Not Your Fault"

A couple of years ago, Montel interviewed a young woman on his show who had some major esteem and confidence issues, stemming from a brutal gang rape. It was a heartbreaking story. Karen was an excellent student, and a loving and helpful young woman of 13 at the time of the attack. She had never given her parents a moment of concern.

Then, one horrifying day, Karen was brutally attacked by a group of teens, and her young life was changed forever. She moved from being a confident, motivated, outgoing girl to an anguished, depressed, direction-less child.

"She started hating her body," her mother, also a guest on the show, recalled. "And hating herself."

The breakdown in Karen's self-esteem set off an avalanche of self-destruction that would last for the next seven years. By the time she turned up on Montel's show, she was 20 and pregnant, and her mother and sister worried that she was suicidal. They feared that she'd try to harm the baby growing inside her, and in the process, harm herself. She had been in and out of treatment for crank, crack, acid, and heroin. She was also bulimic, and prone to violent fits and unexplained emotional outbursts.

At this stage of his television career, counseling teens and families in crisis, Montel had interviewed hundreds of troubled young women in similar straits. He knew the deal, but something about Karen struck a chord. Hearing her story, he could see how everything stemmed from that one brutal incident when she was 13 years old. The proud, positive foundation she and her parents had spent a lifetime building came crashing down in one harrowing moment. And yet, somehow, he felt he could see the sweet, gentle girl that had been hiding inside this mountain of hate and self-loathing for so many years.

To this day, he can't say for certain what made him do it, but Montel reached out to Karen and held her head between his hands and forced her to look closely into his eyes. It was unlike anything he had ever done before, or since—and it still stands out as one of the most memorable and emotional moments in the show's ten-year history. He tearfully pleaded for Karen to let go of the guilt she felt over the rape. "It's not your fault!" he implored, almost yelling.

Somehow, Karen listened. For the first time in seven years, she was ready to face her demons. She had been kicked out of more treatment programs than her mother cared to remember, but this time, something about Karen's pledge to seek help rang true. Indeed, she went directly from Montel's midtown TV studio to a nearby treatment center that often serves as an after-care clinic for guests of the Montel *show.*

This time, therapists were able to reach that place within Karen that had been locked away since the incident. They were able to focus on the rape, instead of the drug use and her diminishing sense of self-worth. The drugs were a symptom of Karen's self-hatred, and if they could get her to confront the problem instead of dance around it, she'd begin to feel better about herself.

Montel kept in close contact with Karen and her family throughout her treatment, and he was happy to bring her back to the program a revitalized young woman. She proudly told the audience that she had been clean since the first taping, and that she was working toward a career as a social worker and rape counselor. She said that if she could help just one person from falling into the same trap that she did, she would feel as if her transformation was complete.

◆ ◆ ◆

···CHAPTER···
THREE

PRACTICAL PRENATAL CARE

Early-childhood planning separates the winners from the losers in our society, and the truly practical parent looks to hit the ground running, based on the theory that it's never too soon to get off on the right foot. Or, as James Brown would say, "Get off on the *good* foot!"

Conversely, it's also never too late to start making an extra effort with your child, but we're here to offer first-resort preventive guidance, not last-ditch corrective measures.

As a parent, you have the power and responsibility to model positive parenting and help your child to become a healthy individual. You are the first line of defense and the front-row cheerleader, all rolled into one, and the key is to start directing your focus in this area when the child is still in the womb. That's right—before the baby is even born. If you want to build strong and proactive character traits in your son or daughter, you must initiate active nurturing as early as possible in your child's life, even during pregnancy. Sound a bit New Age or "out there" for your more conventional thinking?

Well, studies show that the sooner you start providing love, a healthy and positive home environment, and constant support and pride, the more influence you will have on your child's development. And you can't get much sooner than the time right after conception. We're thoroughly convinced that practical early parenting may be the best way to minimize the physical and emotional toll that life's challenges and adversities can take on our young people, and that these efforts should begin the moment you learn you're expecting.

If you happen to be planning a child, or are expecting one now, you're in the best position to think about and employ some test-driven early-parenting techniques, your first steps toward becoming a truly practical parent. We realize that nothing in life is guaranteed, but smart prenatal care dramatically increases the odds of giving birth to a healthy baby. This good health, in turn, provides the foundation for proper emotional and intellectual growth.

Don't Risk the Health of Your Unborn Child

If you're interested or responsible enough to be reading this book, chances are that you already know about the dangers of smoking, drinking, and drug use on the health of the unborn child. Yet some of you may think that drinking wine with dinner, smoking pot on weekends, or even a pack-a-week cigarette habit won't hurt your unborn baby. What garbage! If you're one of these casual drinkers/dopers/smokers, you're hiding behind a "recreational use" label at tremendous risk to the future health of your child. What, specifically, is at risk? How about low birth weight; and birth defects such as missing limbs, asthma, or an oversized head?

Drugs and alcohol also negatively affect the brain development of the fetus, resulting in a host of physiological and intellectual deficits such as conduct disorders, learning disabilities, low IQ, and even mental retardation. If you don't want to go through

the heartache of watching your child struggle and live with a disability or chronic illness—especially one caused by your own
carelessness—then you must set your vices aside for a little while.
Let this pregnancy be your final wake-up call. Take personal
stock. If you've been living anything less than a healthy lifestyle,
now is the time to change—for yourself *and* your child—because
nothing less will do.

We'll talk about eliminating destructive behaviors a little later,
but there's a lot more you can do to improve yourself and protect
your unborn child's health. Let's take the issue of proper nutrition.

Montel: Jeff once promoted a wellness program for women
on a popular New York radio call-in show. He discussed the issue
of obesity and the importance of nutrition and exercise in maintaining appropriate body weight. He thought he was doing a public service, until he received angry calls from black women who
thought he was pushing a white woman's ethic of beauty. That
was the furthest thing from his thinking.

The point, then as now, was that poor nutrition during pregnancy harms the unborn child, no matter what your cultural
notions of beauty are. It is now accepted that good nutrition during pregnancy benefits the health of both the mother and the
baby. Women who eat well and avoid known risks tend to have
fewer complications during pregnancy and labor—and they deliver larger, healthier babies. Full-term babies weighing seven
pounds or more tend to have higher IQs and fewer physical problems than full-term babies weighing less than five-and-a-half
pounds.

If you happen to be overweight, put off dieting until after your
baby is born. Instead, concentrate on moderate exercise and on
improving the quality of the food you eat. Read the labels, and go
natural. And for the time being, at least, let's bury the argument of
what physical beauty really is. Practical parenting dictates that
you've got to eat right. In addition, you've got to exercise and stay

in shape to increase the chances of having a healthier baby. Consult with your OB/GYN or family doctor, and embark on an appropriate diet and exercise plan. If you already exercise, adapt your routine to suit your changing body. Not only will exercise help you and your baby stay healthy, but exercising while pregnant will put you more in touch with your body and all that's happening during this strange and wonderful experience. Exercise keeps both the heart and body healthy and fit, improving posture, and promoting early recovery after delivery.

Certain guidelines for exercising in a healthy manner need to be followed during pregnancy. The American College of Obstetrics and Gynecology recommends the following:

- Drink plenty of water during and after exercise to regulate your baby's body temperature and your own.

- Don't exercise to the point of physical exhaustion. If you start feeling pain, exhaustion, or dizziness during exercise, stop right away.

- Avoid exercise in the supine, or back-lying, position after the first three months of pregnancy.

- Eat more to compensate for the additional calories needed for exercise and a healthy pregnancy.

- Exercise regularly, at least three times a week. This is preferable to working out only once in a while.

A practical exercise routine doesn't have to be complicated, and you shouldn't break the bank on some health-club membership either. Take quick-paced walks to get your legs and heart going. In fact, walking is a great activity for expectant couples to do in tandem, encouraging the equal responsibility of parenting and togetherness.

One of our favorite, most inexpensive, pregnancy-safe regimens is yoga, or any relaxation-based program that incorporates breathing and stress-reduction exercises to enhance your emotional well-being and that of your child's. Women who practice yoga have also been found to have an easier time in childbirth. Try a yoga class specifically tailored for pregnant women, which is also an excellent way to meet other women who are going through the same paces. Being able to share experiences with other practical parents-to-be is incredibly powerful, especially since pregnancy can sometimes feel like a very lonely affair.

Whether in a class or on your own, we strongly recommend establishing a morning and evening routine of yoga-type exercises that are meant to reduce the stress of pregnancy and increase the emotional calm of your unborn child. You can experiment a bit to create a routine that best suits your particular needs, but here are a few suggestions:

Upon waking up, instead of jumping up and starting your day, take a few minutes to practice deep, relaxed breathing. They can be simple, deep breaths or a more formal meditation. Combine this breathing technique with the gentle rubbing of your belly. It's helpful if your partner joins you. This will create a greater bond between the two of you as parents, and with your child. Deep breathing and gentle massage will relax you and the baby, easing you into the day. If you use this morning time to advantage, you will find that you're less irritable and better able to deal with stress. Find pockets of calm throughout the day in which you might repeat your morning routine, even if it's only for a few minutes at a time.

During your deep breathing, conjure up positive images of yourself and your child. Envision your child floating happily inside of you. Picture him or her being born and being held by you. These soothing images will deepen your feelings of calmness, which will, in turn, provide a very relaxed atmosphere for the baby.

Communicate with Your Unborn Child

One of the simplest, most meaningful gifts you can give to yourself and your unborn child is an early dialogue. Start communicating the moment you determine you're pregnant, and set a pattern that will last a lifetime. Studies have shown somewhat conclusively that the fetus can discern sounds and vibrations from within the womb; even more compelling, many experts believe that an unborn child can recognize the mother's voice. And still others maintain that children who are constantly exposed to music during pregnancy perform better in math and science testing throughout their school years.

We say to you: Bring it all on, all the time. Talk to your unborn child. Read to your unborn child. Sing. Get both you and your partner in on the fun, and if there are siblings around, invite them to the party, too. You'll most likely find that these all-important rituals will provide a truly wonderful bonding experience for the whole family.

Let's think outside the box for a moment and consider the scientific benefits of such an undertaking. Researchers, frankly, are fairly split on whether there's any direct benefit to the baby through this type of prenatal stimulation, but as parents, we were willing to roll the dice on this one. We figured, what could it hurt?

Jeff: When Montel's son was just an infant, he was off getting his Mommy the Walkman headphones so she could place them on her belly before Wynter-Grace was born. It became a daily routine. They'd turn the volume up and down, trying to feel the baby's movements in response to the changes in the music. It was a marvelous, nurturing way for the older sibling to reach back and connect with his soon-to-be-born baby sister, and a way to forge a feeling of family like no other.

Even more important, it was a way to get the mind of that unborn child working, and responding to new sets of stimuli.

How many times have you heard well-meaning aunts and grand-mothers tell a roomful of well-meaning visitors to keep their voices down, so as not to disturb the expectant mother and her unborn child? If you ask us, people should speak in normal tones around the pregnant mother at all times—the pregnant mother, especially. There'll be plenty of time for whispering after the child is born. Speak plainly. Assume the child can hear, because there's enough research to support that assumption. We even found one study that placed a newborn baby in a crib, surrounded that crib with the baby's mother and six imposters, and watched as the infant turned his head toward his mother's voice almost every time. So, yes, we are true believers in prenatal education.

Montel: And Jeff has trumpeted the benefits of prenatal education to every expectant parent he's worked with in therapy.

For the disbelievers among you, there's even a controversial study that concludes that babies can begin to process information from the outside world by the seventh day of conception! More recent mainstream studies promote prenatal stimulation through parenting activities such as reading to the fetus, which is viewed as being vitally important for the growing brain to continue its development. Music played a big part in both of our households during pregnancy—in part because we both love music, but also because of testing that reported higher IQs for children exposed to a variety of musical stimulation through the womb. Incidentally, this exposure to music should continue throughout infancy, incorporating a broad range of musical styles. If your children listen to a variety of music every day, their math and science aptitude will soar, as their spatial reasoning and schematic comprehension increase.

Jeff: Montel can even remember watching a Discovery Channel documentary on the subject while his wife Grace was pregnant with their son. The documentary showed an MRI of the brain of a one-year-old infant who had been exposed to an hour of classical music every day of his little life. That image was contrasted with a composite MRI from infants who hadn't been formally exposed to music, and you could actually see the areas of enhanced development. The thing was lit up like a Christmas tree!

We've even found a validating study that nicely straddles our two areas of expertise: psychology and television. Researcher Peter G. Hepper, reporting in the *Irish Journal of Psychology* (1991), studied fetuses two to four days old that had been exposed on a nearly daily basis to the theme song from of a popular television program while their mothers were pregnant. When the same tune was played after birth, the babies exhibited changes in heart rate and movement, which seemed to indicate that learning can happen *before* birth, even though it doesn't end there. There are other arguments for the child receiving both prenatal and after-birth music stimulation and education. Additional research has shown a causal relationship between exposure to music and abstract post-birth reasoning ability, and behavior scientists now believe that music has many benefits for children beyond those within the arena of music itself. Music is thought to contribute to the development of intellectual, motor, and social abilities.

Creating a Safe Home Environment

Practical prenatal preparedness naturally extends to the baby's first home—which, after all, can be seen as an extension of the mother's womb. The home is the place where the child will grow and live with parents, family, and friends. We don't care if it's a palatial mansion or a tiny, nothing-special apartment, the home is the foundation of love and belonging, the shelter from the storm, the place where our children develop the courage and strength to venture out into the world. During the early years of life, this most important place will help shape a child's personality and build character. Naturally, a negative environment can destroy the psychological potential and self-esteem of even the most emotionally resilient child.

As practical parents, it is within our power to build a home environment that will bring out the best in our children, especially during infancy. A healthy home will communicate healthy ideals, such as self-discipline and pride. Think back to your own anecdotal experiences for proof of this one. Remember the troubled kids you knew who may have lived in uncertain environments? The kids whose homes were dirty, overcrowded, or chaotic were often cast as victims, perhaps because they didn't develop a proper sense of personal boundaries. Others had a tough time finishing high school, or turned to drugs and alcohol to help get themselves through their troubled days and nights. Many in our acquaintance continued in the cycle of poverty and went on public assistance as soon as they were of legal age, even if they were able-bodied.

But even in our poorest ghettos, there are success stories— stories of children who were raised in clean, orderly households where self-esteem, discipline, and love were the order of the day. What this means is that a positive and healthy home environment is not based on material possessions or wealth, but on the ability and desire of parents to take control and establish a home that will benefit the child until he or she leaves the nest.

What can you do to create a healthy home environment that will enrich your newborn physically and psychologically and provide the foundation that will contribute to success in life? Ideally, you would want to create this environment before conception, but in all cases, you should have your house in order by the time you bring your child home from the hospital. On the simplest level, make sure your home is free from physical dangers and structural problems that could hurt your baby. There should be guards on your apartment windows, socket covers, and no exposed electrical wires or circuits.

Try to think of everything. A great way to do this is to actually get down on all fours and look at your home from a child's perspective. Crawl around for a while, and determine where a baby might get into trouble. An antique linen chest that's been in your family for generations might seem harmless now, but if a small child can lift the lid and crawl inside, you might want to think about putting the heirloom in storage until the child is older. One item that usually escapes everyone's attention is the electrical cord running from your floor or table lamp. (We know, because it escaped ours!) A gentle tug by a tiny hand can bring that lamp rocketing to the floor.

Prescription drugs should be stored on a high shelf, in securely fastened childproof bottles. Even aspirin and over-the-counter medications should be out of reach. Ideally, these items should be locked up, but that's usually not practical. Hide them if you can, and always know what's on hand. If you see an open bottle lying around, nearly empty, you'll need to know how many pills were inside originally. Similarly, household poisons such as detergents, turpentine, insect sprays, and paints should be stored in a safe place. Guns should not be kept *at all* in homes with small children. We're firm on this one, across the board, although we recognize that some of you will have a different opinion. If you choose to keep a weapon, you must keep it unloaded, *in a locked cabinet.*

Try to remember how resourceful and nosy you were as a child. As kids, we knew every nook and cranny in our homes, and there was little chance of anything being hidden without our knowing about it. With this in mind, teach your children what guns can do, and know that they'll still probably want to check them out for themselves. Wherever you hide your weapons, make sure the ammunition is kept under separate lock and key, in a completely different part of the house—and relocate the entire arsenal on a fairly regular basis.

Make sure you have smoke and carbon monoxide detectors installed throughout your home, perhaps even a full-scale fire alarm if it's a private house. The cost is minimal, and even a few seconds' warning can save lives. Make sure the alarm is working properly and checked regularly. We've all heard too many horror stories of well-meaning parents who removed the batteries from a faulty device to quiet an intermittent signal, and never got around to having it repaired until tragedy hit. Let's be especially diligent on this one, so we don't have to hear tragic stories like this anymore.

Many older homes and apartments should be checked for lead paint and asbestos. Babies are extremely oral—they put everything into their mouths. As the paint flakes off a wall, many children ingest it, become sick, and can eventually suffer brain damage, leading to attention deficit disorder (ADD), as well as developmental and other learning disabilities. Have your home inspected by a licensed contractor or professional painter to determine what kind of paint you have and whether it is lead-based. If it is, then you must have the paint stripped. If lead-free paint is chipped and peeling, you should spring for a new coat as well.

Pests are also a nagging problem in many older buildings—and in some new ones as well. No, we're not suggesting that you kick your spouse out on the curb, but if you have a bonafide pest or rodent problem—the kind people spray for—get to work on it right away, since it will directly affect the health of your child. Mice droppings in food can be poisonous. Epidemiologists now believe that roaches and roach dirt can cause an allergic reaction in children, resulting in asthma. It has been theorized that the Bronx, New York, has the largest number of childhood cases of asthma in the country because of its excessive pest infestation.

And then there are those pests on the other side of your apartment walls. Noisy neighbors will finally have to be dealt with upon the birth of your child. You know, the guy who cranks his music at 11:00 P.M. every weeknight. If you've been able to grin and bear it, now is the time to explain as peacefully as you can that a baby will soon be living in your home. Have the conversation now, before your patience is worn thin. Ask, in your most neighborly tone, if your neighbor might cooperate and turn the volume down after a certain hour, preferably around seven or eight in the evening. Most pediatricians agree that during infancy, a child should be put to bed no later than eight o'clock. This early bedtime will assure a proper sleep cycle, which will allow for the baby's rest, and optimum growth. Most neighbors will be happy to accommodate your reasonable request—that is, if you make sure to present it reasonably.

If there's anyone in your home who smokes or drinks, now may be the best time to establish house rules with regard to smoking outdoors and not drinking excessively in front of the baby or other children. Secondhand smoke is very bad for adults, but it is even more insidious to a developing child. It can cause lower body weight, can stunt growth, and handicap intellectual potential. And just as important, your smoking and drinking may become imprinted in your child's mind, perhaps increasing the chances that he or she will find it natural to smoke or drink later in life.

And finally, it's essential that your home be kept clean, neat, and as germ free as possible, especially for the baby's first year, when his or her immune system may not be totally developed. Moreover, there are many emotional benefits that the baby can also derive from good hygienic practices, such as responsibility, discipline, and the willingness to take pride in his or her appearance. Clean-up times should quickly become part of the daily routine—putting toys away after playtime, making beds, placing soiled clothes in the hamper, and other easy tasks that are within a child's ability. But clean-up times will always be an afterthought if you don't do your part to establish an orderly environment. As the child continues to mature, this self-discipline will translate into such behaviors as doing homework assignments neatly and on time.

Imposing structure in an orderly home will directly affect your children's habits with regard to being steadfast and having pride in whatever they accomplish. Remember, you, the parents, are your children's greatest teachers and role models, and if you have an indifferent attitude about performing tasks, your children will follow suit.

A Shift in Priorities

Shannon, a 29-year-old graphic designer, had been coming to therapy for years to discuss issues related to her stormy upbringing. Her parents drank and had volatile tempers. They set the kind of inconsistent examples that left Shannon thinking that she'd never start a family of her own because she was so afraid of repeating the very same mistakes.

While in therapy, Shannon discovered that she was approximately three weeks pregnant, from a casual relationship with a friend. She decided she wanted to have the baby but didn't want to marry the father. It was too soon, Shannon thought, for them to be together as a couple, and it didn't seem practical to get together now, with a kind of gun to their heads.

But there was another kind of gun to Shannon's head, and she recognized it and responded to it right away. Because of the tension in her relationship with her parents, and due to a general lack of self-esteem, Shannon had become a moderate drinker and a heavy smoker. She had talked about trying to quit in therapy, before becoming pregnant, but she was never able to push herself into specific treatment. There was never any kind of now-or-never need. She was comfortable talking about this issue, and acknowledging it, but she said that she enjoyed smoking too much to give it up, and she didn't see that her drinking had really reached any kind of problem stage.

Yet, upon hearing of her pregnancy, Shannon took a different viewpoint. She was smart enough, and emotionally connected enough, to realize that her bad habits would get in the way of her baby's good health. Even her lifestyle, the kind that had her sleeping with "friends" she would never consider as partners, would have to change. Don't misunderstand—she wasn't the sort of person who had multiple sex partners, nor was she the type of woman who flitted in and out of relationships as the mood suited her, but if you're about to become a parent, any number more than one is multiple, right?

Shannon immediately enrolled in a smoking-cessation group and joined Alcoholics Anonymous (AA). It was never a question of "should she" or "shouldn't she." It was simply something that needed to be done.

As Jeff recalls, this piece of the puzzle wasn't even discussed in therapy. The rest of what Shannon needed to accomplish was more difficult, because it took her down a less concrete path. See, Shannon also knew that being a healthy parent meant working through her anger with her own parents. It was what had brought her into therapy in the first place, even though after several years she had made little progress in this area. With the pregnancy, however, it was as if a light switched on in Shannon's head. She saw things differently—the world, her parents—everything. She came to understand that different parents have different parenting styles, which helped her start to forgive her parents and develop a new identity that she could take into her own role as a mother.

This last breakthrough was key to Shannon's development and preparation for single parenthood. Her good physical health was a given, and she had no doubts that her smoking and AA experiences would prove to be fruitful. But more than that, she was plugged in enough to realize that her unborn child would experience the negative feelings she was carrying around inside her, and she wanted to make a thorough emotional housecleaning as well. Shannon needed to come to terms with some of the decisions her parents had made when she was a child. She needed to find a way to forgive them. She needed to accept that she could find her own way as a parent, without mirroring the behaviors she'd been exposed to as a child.

Clearly, Shannon was surprised by her pregnancy, but that child was in no way unwanted. Indeed, it's almost possible to look on that baby as Shannon's life preserver, because it took an unplanned pregnancy to shake loose some of the issues she'd been grappling with for years. She knew that to give her baby every advantage, she would also have to take every advantage for herself.

Shannon's awakening extended to her love life as well, as she and the baby's father vowed to let their relationship find its own way. They weren't ready for marriage, but they were ready to make a commitment to each other and to their unborn child. Good for them. And good for the baby.

Jump ahead a couple years, and we're happy to report that mother and child are doing fine. Shannon no longer drinks or smokes, and she is the proud, devoted mother of a beautiful, healthy baby boy. Shannon never married the baby's father, we should mention, but they remain in each other's lives as parenting partners and good friends.

Different people respond differently to different wake-up calls. Some folks hit the snooze button and hope that their problems go away before the darn thing rings again. In Shannon's case, she took the call seriously. In an ideal world, we would all clean house emotionally and physically before conceiving a child, but that's not always possible. Sometimes we can't even conceive of conceiving a child. But in our less-than-ideal world, we should celebrate those who rise up, against seemingly overwhelming odds, and reinvent themselves for the benefit of their children.

◆ ◆ ◆

···CHAPTER···
FOUR

PRACTICAL ACCESSORIES

Your newborn is like a sponge that's absorbing all sorts of new and compelling information. Indeed, the period from birth to age three is the optimal time for learning, when the baby's brain cells are in the process of rapid development, and when the child experiences many things for the first time. Practical parents should, therefore, try to create as stimulating an environment as possible—as soon as possible—to promote their child's intellectual growth, and the best place to start is with the baby's immediate surroundings.

Make Room for Baby

For many of you, making room will mean a nursery—that extra space you figured you might someday need for something other than your old pull-out couch, your exercise bicycle, and your college textbooks. For others, it might mean a quiet corner of the room you share with your partner. In households with older children, it might even require a doubling- or tripling-up in an existing kid-friendly place. (As far as we can determine, no one markets a line of bunk-cribs, so you'll have to be resourceful if you're dealing with cramped spaces.) In all circumstances, however, the new baby will require an out-of-the-way, brightly colored space to call his or her own.

Now, about those bright colors. We don't know about you, but we're thinking that the old pink-for-girls, blue-for-boys scheme has been pretty much played out. In fact, we haven't seen a single piece of data to suggest that a little girl's room should be decorated in pinks, or that a little boy's room should be decorated in blues. To our thinking, if you blue-pink your brain, you will blue-pink your children, and when you do that, you limit how your kids might look at the world. You saddle them with preset notions of what they should respond to and what they should become. So stop it before it starts, and take that blue paint back to the hardware store and trade it in for some bright, gender-neutral colors. Later on, if your son tells you that blue is his favorite color, you can redecorate; if your daughter turns out to have a thing for pink lace and frills, then let it be *her* decision. If she's *feeling* blue, then let that be okay, too.

For now, though, go with variety, and keep things vibrant. And realize that for every study we haven't seen advocating blue or pink, we've seen compelling evidence to suggest that children confined to a dark, single-colored space for the first several months of their lives will be more likely to develop color blindness than children presented with multicolored, bright patterns. (If you're determined to go with a blue theme, then, at least go with *light* blue!)

We don't mean to assume that every newborn will have his or her own room. Rich or poor, this is a rather large assumption, and there's nothing wrong with carving out some space in your own bedroom or in a common area such as a living room. It's important, however, that the space be clearly defined and child-specific. If you've got more than one child sharing space in an alcove off the dining room, be sure to decorate each sleeping area with small, personal touches. Almost any space will do, especially in the first months of a newborn's life—before the child starts to move about and take up more room than you ever thought possible. We know of one resourceful family that turned a vented, walk-in closet into a circus-themed mini-nursery, which their child comfortably and happily called his own for years.

For the first few weeks, you'll most likely be sleeping with the child in your room anyway—he or she will be in a carriage, or in a bassinet at the foot of your bed. Typically, nursing mothers want to keep the child nearby for those at-first gratifying, but soon enough sleep-depriving, nighttime feedings. We did the same. From a mother's perspective, there's nothing as convenient as rolling over and dropping a breast and sleeping through. Be careful, though, not to fall into a deep sleep while your infant child is in bed with you. You put the baby in jeopardy. Your body at rest will likely fail to recognize the baby's movements, and possibly regard the child like a small pillow. So, there's definitely a safety issue here, but more than that, there's an emotional issue that continues to confound mental-health professionals.

Psychologists and psychiatrists are pretty much split on this one, so we'll give you our two cents (actually, four cents—two for each of us) to confuse you even further. We say, work against the nurturing impulse to take your newborn into bed with you—but don't sweat it if you stray from your better judgment from time to time. Make it the exception and not the rule. Napping together is okay, but steer clear of any middle-of-the-night habits that might be tough to break. As your child gets older, nightmares and stomach bugs might warrant a night or two in your bed, but do what you can to give your child his or her own space.

Throw away the expert opinions, and think this one through for yourself. What are you gaining by sleeping with your child? What is the child gaining? Sure, it's fulfilling and nurturing and beautiful and natural. Good things, all. But break it down and you'll see that you're trading convenience for early independence. A child left to cry and possibly comfort him- or herself back to

sleep is well ahead of the child who's picked up at the first out-
burst and cradled by a parent. You're thwarting the baby's autonomy, at an age where that autonomy is fundamental. It's an age
of discovery—every moment of every day there's something
new—and if you get in the way of a child's ability to explore the
world, you get in the way of the child's development.

Another great argument against the child-in-the-parents' bed
model is the wedge it can place between the mother and father.
Literally. Just as the child wants to get at the mother's breast, so
does the father! We hate to be crass about it, but that's what it
comes down to. (Jeff sees it all the time in his practice). A tension
grows in the relationship between the new mother and the new
father, and it's almost always possible to connect that tension to
what's going on with the child at night. The family should return
to business-as-usual as soon as possible after the new arrival. If it
takes some time restoring intimacy into the equation, don't let it
be *directly* because of the baby. (Okay, we all know that, in one
way or another, it will have *everything* to do with the baby, but
there's no reason to place the kid in the middle in any kind of
concrete way.)

Help Yourself, and Help Your Baby

Children should have their own place to sleep, their own
place to thrive, and parents should have their privacy. Blur the
boundaries at your own risk. Too often, the mother gives up
everything she once was and throws a thousand percent into rais-
ing that infant, when a hundred percent would be more than
enough. It's the mother with the baby in her bed who gets hit
hardest with those initial bouts of postpartum psychosis or depression, and the mother with the baby constantly on her hip who
complains the loudest about not having any kind of life now that
there's a kid in the picture. And it's the child who was overnur-
tured who walks around afraid of his own shadow, and who gets

teased by his classmates for being a "Mama's boy," or a sissy.

You cut the umbilical cord in the delivery room, but you're still connected, and you've got to begin emotionally cutting those ties as soon as possible. Start slowly, but make the effort. And let the father do some of the heavy lifting—especially in the middle of the night. Sure, the nursing mother has to have a role, but the father can lift his butt out of bed, collect the crying child from the nursery, change a diaper, and deliver the baby to the mother. Then, after the feeding, the father can rock the child back to sleep. Even better, nursing mothers should consider purchasing a breast pump, which allows them to express and store a certain amount of milk each day, for those times when she's unavailable to feed the child—or, for those times when she's determined to get some sleep. The expense is minimal, there are a number of fine models available, and we've found these to be enormously liberating little devices.

Keep in mind that you can safely store breast milk for up to 12 hours in the refrigerator, after which you're better off tossing what's left and pumping some more. Even at 12 hours, you sacrifice some of the nutritional benefits of the straight-from-the-source stuff—but it's worth the trade-off for one or two bottle feedings over a 24-hour period. Pediatricians assure us that the nursing baby will still get everything she needs from Mom throughout the rest of the day.

Some of the more elaborately stocked baby stores will feature one of the silliest items we've seen for new parents—a bottle-holding harness, designed to be worn by the father almost like a brassiere, with a tiny holster at each breast for a baby bottle. Come on! We're not here to slam some entrepreneur's ability to make a buck, but let's learn to think for ourselves a little bit.

We set this down, then, as a warning to you parents to keep your senses about you and trust your instincts. Just because you're new parents, it doesn't mean that you have to scarf up every product these people think to sell you. Dads, it's more than enough to carry that child in your own arms, hold that supplemental bottle in your own hand, and do the job yourself. You've got all the tools you need—no bells and whistles required.

If you make the personal choice to avoid these supplemental feedings, find ways to include the father in the process just the same. When we were kids, this was the mother's job, plain and simple, but times have changed. If Mom's got to get up, then Dad's got to get up. Stay close. Become a family. And make sure the baby starts to see the two of you there, together, as much as possible. Show the baby from the earliest possible moment that there are two people who love him or her very much. If there are older siblings around, include them in these feedings, too—as long as they're not so much of a distraction that the baby can't focus on the task at hand. Be there for your newborn at this most important part of the day.

As fathers, we weren't thrilled about giving up those feeding times and the special bond that comes along with it, so we found ways to compensate in order to be a part of the process. We even rearranged our work schedules to match our availability to feeding time. Also, one of the great ways in which a doting father can co-opt some intimate time with a nursing newborn is to stake a claim on bathtime. (Those nursing mothers get all the props!)

Jeff: Montel made a daily habit of this with his two youngest children, and it became one of those joyous, formative bonds that will hopefully last a lifetime. To this day, there's a special connection they all feel around the water, and Montel likes to think that it flows in some way from those early bathtime rituals.

So, to you new fathers out there, think a little outside the box and claim some intimate territory of your own, because in the care-and-feeding department, there aren't too many jobs to go around.

Buying for Baby

We've shifted, somewhat, from the main focus of this chapter, but here again, as in everything else, you'll want to do things in moderation. Keep things simple on your first couple of trips to the baby supply store. You'll want to place a mobile or some other stimuli atop and around your child's crib or bassinet, and here the trend has been toward black and white, based on research that tells us that newborns are unable to discern colors for the first few weeks. Stroll through any baby store and you'll find aisle upon aisle of black-and-white mobiles, crib bumpers, pillows, and stuffed animals. That's fine for the first two or three weeks, but why not make room for some of the brighter yellows and reds and greens as soon as possible?

Texture, we've found, is another sensation that's too often ignored by young parents, but here again, there are a number of targeted products on the market that play to the latest research. The fact is, if you want to help develop *all* of your baby's senses, the best place to start is *touch*. Crib sheets, blankets, and bumpers don't all have to be made of the same material. Cotton is fine, and perhaps best for constant contact against the baby's skin, but you can find some delightful, crib-friendly items in corduroy and dimpled fabric to offer the newborn an interesting textural contrast. A number of manufacturers make a full line of touchable crib accessories that include shiny plastics, rough scratch pads, and downy cottons, because healthy babies need to become sensitized to touch at the earliest possible age.

One of the biggest baby-store sellers is the pacifier, but as parents, we avoided those suckers like the plague—and as far as we could ever tell, our kids never missed them. The theory behind pacifiers is presumably sound: Fussy babies can sometimes by comforted by replicating the sucking motion against the nipple, but you'd never know it from the way these things are deployed. The unmistakable cartoon image of Bart Simpson's baby sister, sucking away on her plug, is a dead-on satire of our hectic lifestyles, where parents are too busy to take the time to comfort their children the old-fashioned way—or to feed them when they're hungry. Invariably, you'll see some harried parent plugging one of those things into a child's mouth at the first sign of fussing, and leave it there until it falls out or becomes permanently suctioned across the child's lips and needs to be surgically removed.

We know a number of intelligent people who've used the pacifier sparingly—to help an overtired child drop off to sleep, for example—and many who've sworn that it was the single best defense against the less-desirable thumb-sucking, but we chose to go another way. This is one of those areas where it's hard to see a definitive right or wrong, and we leave it to you to figure out the method that works best for your family, but we each felt we could do better without relying on some false consolation. We believed that it was worth the trouble to strive for the real deal, and help our children develop tools to comfort themselves.

And realize, we came to this shared conclusion separately— before we even met and decided to put our heads together on these parenting issues. Our feeling was that the pacifier was designed to pacify the parent, not the child. That constant sucking motion is not natural, and about all it does at first is fool hungry children into thinking they're being fed. Over time, it almost becomes a Pavlovian response. Stick it in, shut up. Pull it out, cry. Stick it in, shut up. Pull it out, cry.

Granted, there are times when a child needs to suck on something other than the mother's breast or a bottle—when teething, for example—but there are a number of teething rings on the market that do the job far better than a nipple-shaped pacifier. There are also certain topical medications you can use to ease a child's discomfort when teething. And there's the old standby—a parent's finger (well washed, of course!). This last suggestion is far more effective than the child's own thumb, because you can readily remove it at will.

Montel: Another baby-store staple you weren't likely to find at Jeff's house was a stroller. He strongly believes that an over-reliance on the stroller is detrimental to both parent and child—and to the relationship they're forging together.

To be sure, a stroller is a necessary accessory up until your children learn to walk, but after that, our feeling is that it gets in the way more than it helps. It sends a negative message to children that they can't keep up!—and it certainly doesn't do much to foster leg strength, confidence, or self-reliance. Better to shorten your walks to age-appropriate distances so that your children might accompany you than to push them along. Children who are sitting still, shielded from view by canopies, don't develop emotionally at the same pace as children out in the open air, moving along on their own power. Plus, facing forward like that, away from the parent, places the child on a relatively solitary journey; there's little opportunity for parent-child interaction, which essentially reduces the walk to an upper-body exercise for adults only, and a missed opportunity for some parent-child bonding in the great outdoors.

Naturally, there are times in the life of a young family when a stroller is warranted—even for a healthy four- or five-year-old. A trip to the zoo or amusement park is hardly manageable on a small child's little legs, and here, a "moving rest stop" in a rented stroller will prolong your time at whatever attraction it is you're touring, saving back-weary parents a trip to the chiropractor the following morning.

Our advice, then, is to quit the stroller once the child learns to walk. Cold turkey. In that transitional stage between toddling and walking, there will almost always be a strong enough set of adult shoulders around to get you through the rough patches. Allow your child the comfort of a free ride, and you'll likely find that it's a tough habit to break—for both of you.

Approach your trips to the baby store like an anthropologist exploring some lost civilization. Check out the products, and think about what's behind them and what you might do to improve them. Get what you need, and borrow the rest. All things being equal, you could probably achieve some of the same results with items you've already got lying around the house. We read somewhere that tennis star Andre Agassi's parents strung a tennis ball across his crib with a piece of yarn, thereby encouraging the development of the future tennis pro's eye-hand coordination. That's great—and there's no reason why you can't spend a little time on this and come up with some creative ideas of your own.

There are also some wonderful computer programs that can help you build custom puzzles using family photos; and you can make a fun, proactive spinning mobile with any number of items you might find in your kitchen utensil drawer. Educational toys, especially the interactive models that talk and play music, will develop attention and focusing skills, as well as enhance problem-solving skills, but never underestimate the power of a good old-fashioned story made up out of thin air. Puppets will help give your stories a voice, and if you don't feel like dropping a couple hundred bucks for a top-of-the-line marionette, dig an old sock out of your drawer, slap some fabric on for a mouth and eyes, and start the show.

If you share your love of learning, reading, and creative thinking with your children, it won't matter which packaged items you bring home from the store. What matters will be the extra efforts you make to engage your children, and to get them to expand their boundaries. Feed your children's intellect and curiosity, but at the same time, lay down a pattern of learning that will last a lifetime.

Too Close for Comfort

This parenting business can be hard, especially the first time out of the gate. And for many new parents, this sleeping-in-the-bed confusion can be one of the toughest dilemmas. Everybody seems to do it, yet many warn against it. In some cultures, it's a way of life; in ours, it's set out as some sort of road to ruin . . . and there seems to be precious little middle ground.

James, age 25; and Shirley, age 22, came to Jeff in couples therapy over this one issue. Actually, there was a whole lot going on, but you could draw a line from virtually every problem in their marriage, every piece of tension, to the arrival of their six-month-old son. Shirley had the baby sleeping in their bed every day and night. It wasn't a matter of not having a big enough place for the child to have his own room, nor was it a matter of not being able to afford a crib or outfit a nursery. It came down to Shirley's notion of motherhood, which held that a good mother did not separate from her child—even if it meant abandoning her husband.

It had gotten to the point where there was virtually no communication between James and Shirley, yet mounds of resentment existed. Most of the bitterness flowed from James to Shirley, because even she later admitted that she was too caught up in the baby to resent anything James may or may not have been doing. She didn't even have it in her to resent James's tendency to not take on his share of the parenting load. This was probably because she was such a hands-on mother that it had to be her *hands on the child, and not her husband's. Whatever was going on between them as husband and wife, or whatever was not going on between them, Shirley just didn't notice. One thing was for sure, though: They had no sex life. From James's perspective, it was because there was no opportunity; from Shirley's, it was because there was no need.*

It was a classic case of over-involvement on the mother's behalf, but it was also perfectly understandable. It happens all the time. We know, because we see it occur regularly. It even happened to each of us, to a degree, back when we were new parents. It's like a rite of passage that you just have to get through. You do this by acknowledging that it's basically a simple problem with a simple solution: communication. Sometimes it takes a therapist or some other objective third party to help reopen those lines of communication, but this is a problem that couples can work on themselves. All they need to do is talk about it.

The time to talk about it, preferably, is before the baby is born, because you don't want all of this anger and resentment spilling over into your interactions with the child. But even if that time has passed, it's not too late. Just start talking—to each other, naturally, but also to yourselves. Be honest about your feelings.

By doing just that, Shirley was able to see that it was possible to be a mother and a wife without guilt. James could express his love and devotion to the baby and to Shirley without feeling as though he had to play one against the other. Without communication, it had always seemed an either-or proposition, this baby business, but as long as they could talk about things and keep the lines open, there was no limit to their capacity to compromise.

There was, however, a real limit to the size of their bed, and Jeff was firm about getting the baby into his own crib. He pointed out the harmful effects on the baby, the spoiling, the potential for lack of independence and maturational growth; and when he put the argument in those terms, Shirley came around. Soon, Shirley and James became intimate again, and their bed became their shared personal space. There was still room for the baby in that space—on an occasional, limited basis—but he had his own personal space in his own room down the hall.

One of the great side benefits to this plan was the relationship James was able to forge with his son. He had come into therapy hoping to reclaim the relationship he felt he had lost with his wife, but he had never been able to bond with the baby through all that resentment and anger. The whole father-son relationship was set aside. Plus, there was no room for it, with all of Shirley's constant doting. All it took was a couple step backs for Shirley to allow James his couple steps forward, and when this new family met in the middle, it made all the difference in the world.

◆ ◆ ◆

···CHAPTER···
FIVE

THE PRACTICAL DIFFERENCES BETWEEN BOYS AND GIRLS

Have you ever noticed that we make things harder on ourselves than they need to be? As parents, partners, consumers, colleagues . . . whatever it is, we've set things up so that we must constantly look over our shoulders and worry if we're doing the *right* thing instead of what just *feels* right.

Indeed, we live in a time of such political and gender-based correctness that a great deal of the parenting literature goes out of its way to neutralize the developmental differences between boys and girls, and we begin our discussion on this all-important issue wondering if we should even bother.

Why wonder? Well, as you've no doubt noticed if you've read with us to this point, this book is *not* set up to offer extensive research and commentary on any one issue. It's not any kind of end-all or last word. It's simply meant to get you thinking practically as parents—to get you jump-started and looking at your relationships with your children in a whole new way.

If you need to focus specifically on one problem, or on one

stage of the parenting process, we'll try to set you off with enough tools and the kind of practical mind-set you'll need to learn more. And, hopefully, you'll apply these new skills on behalf of your children.

Here, we're going to discuss the difference between boys and girls, the various approaches you'll need to take with your daughters and your sons in diverse situations. We've checked out the available research on this controversial topic, and the prevailing wisdom, and we've made what we like to think is an intelligent decision: We're going to throw all of that stuff out the door and go with our guts, because that's what *we* did as parents, and that's what *you'll* likely do when the time comes to split hairs on this issue.

The trend over the past several years has been to treat boys and girls the same. Separate but equal. Send our daughters the message that they can compete on the same field as boys, that they can even play in the same game. Tell our sons that they can open up to their friends and share their feelings. Create an open, accepting environment where boys will be boys, and girls will be girls—and, sometimes, girls will be boys, and boys will be girls. Well, our take on this trend is that it's bunk. Obviously, boys and girls are anatomically different, but those differences extend throughout their makeup. Their little brains function differently, and we practical parents need to keep this in mind as we guide them through their early development.

Later on, once our gender-driven society takes them out for a spin, they'll send us signals on how they'd like to be treated, chromosomally speaking. We're talking about the first couple of years. Before puberty and other signs of maturation kick in, before our cultural expectations have a chance to take root, you'll see some real differences that you'll need to embrace. Here's just one example: Little girls have an easier time developing musically and artistically than little boys. That's just the way they're wired. That doesn't mean you can't turn out a male violin prodigy, or a tone-deaf female who can't draw her way out of a paper bag, but it does mean that girls are more inclined in this area. Put a bunch of kids in a room and ask them to draw a picture of a house, and what will you get back? The little boys will draw blocklike variations on a theme, and the little girls might add windows, curtains, and maybe a flower garden out in front, alongside a path leading up to the house from the street.

It all seems too clear, and yet it's taken us to the year 2000 to recognize that the combustible differences in our estrogen and testosterone levels leave us all predisposed to certain types of behavior at certain stages in our development. We've worked hard to neuter our children in these types of discussions, to where we approach them in gender-neutral ways, but our kids are not androgynous. They're just not. They might make specific, gender-related choices as they get older, but from the outset, we see that they're predisposed toward certain types of behavior.

Jeff: Montel's kids are cases in point. Wynter-Grace, at age five, would wear a dress to the playground if given the choice. She doesn't like to get dirty. Montel II could live in the mud half the day and not even think about it. He doesn't care what he looks like. Now there are those of you who might suggest that Wynter-Grace is possibly mirroring her mother on this one, and that Montel II is possibly mirroring his dad—or perhaps that each child is reflecting some of the cultural expectations we place on our children. But the truth is that this is how these kids were from the moment they were born, before any mirroring or preconceptions had a chance to take hold. As an infant, Montel II liked to get down and dirty; he was a roll-around-in-the-sand kind of kid. Wynter-Grace was tentative around a mess and tended to get all fussy if things weren't just so.

Montel: It was the same with Jeff's kids. His daughter, Q'vanaa, was all sugar and lace; and his son, Puma, was into rocks and insects and dirt—an obsession he most certainly didn't get from his father, a man who is probably listed in most dictionaries under "obsessive/compulsive neat freak."

As they've grown up, some of their little boy-isms and their little girl-isms can be traced more to our cultural expectations, but there's no denying them. Montel II greets people with a hard-as-he-can high-five; Wynter-Grace with a shy smile. He's rough and tumble; she's soft and frilly. That's to be expected, we suppose, but why is it that we instill in certain personality traits a gender-specific bias? Why is sensitivity a female trait? Why are boys physically competitive? Why is aggressiveness celebrated in a little boy and eschewed in a little girl? It even infects the language. A sensitive boy is always spoken of in qualified terms: "He's very sensitive—for a boy." A competitive girl, in the same way: "She's very competitive—for a girl."

We Don't Need to Program Our Children

Why do we socialize our children along these proscribed lines? Why can't our little girls be more aggressive, and our little boys more compassionate? Well, the truth is, they can . . . *if* we let them, and *if* we decide not to program them or force them. The key is to open up our hearts and our minds enough so that *all* of our children have the freedom to explore the full range of their personalities. Sure, boys might be more inclined in one way, and girls more inclined in another, but with a gentle push from Mom and Dad, they can be whatever they want to be, whatever they were meant to be.

But let's never lose sight of the fact that, at the root of it all, what our little boys and our little girls were meant to be was *different*. There always has been and always will be certain basic differences between the sexes, and these differences manifest themselves in all kinds of ways. Authorities on youth coaching, for example, will tell you that you must take a separate approach with girls than with boys. For a team sport like soccer, many girls place the highest value on team unity and camaraderie, on feeling part of a whole, while boys might emphasize skills and drills that promote teamwork. We know of one youth coach who takes his daughter's team out for pizza *before* the season begins as a means of knitting the girls together as a group; and his son's team out for pizza *after* the season ends as a final celebration and to let them burn off steam.

So, absolutely, there are differences. Girls learn from their mistakes; boys take some time getting the point. Girls are more likely to by swayed by what they think their friends are saying; boys are more likely to be swayed by what they think their friends are *thinking*. Girls will be more diligent in their schoolwork; boys will be tempted to get by on as little work as possible. Girls are more trusting; boys are less forgiving. Girls are tentative; boys are reckless. Think back to every gender-based cliché you've collected in your life, and realize that some of them are rooted in truth. What are little girls made of? Sugar and spice and everything nice? And boys? Snakes and snails and puppy-dog's tails?

Okay, so it's a hit-or-miss equation, but let's work on being a little more accepting of the variations between the sexes. In the rush to claim equality, we've let some of these important differences fall through the cracks. More accurately, we've washed over them to where we hope not to recognize them. We're not suggesting that when you take your newborns home from the hospital you place trucks in your son's crib and dolls in your daughter's. But we *are* suggesting that you keep an open mind. And keep your eyes open, too, to what your children are showing you through their behavior. Watch them, see where they gravitate, and avoid the impulse to counter-program their interests if a child seems *too* masculine or *too* feminine.

Jeff: Let's recognize, too, that our children will naturally emulate the parent of like gender—in matters of style *and* personality. One of the hardest things for Montel to accept was when his two oldest daughters went through puberty, because they wanted nothing to do with him. They shut him out of every new thing that was going on in their lives, and every new development that was taking place with their bodies, because they had all the sounding board they needed in their mother. He wanted desperately to be able to talk with them, but they were too embarrassed, when they were in the middle of everything, to come to him with these issues. This was a time when they needed their mother, and Montel had to accept that.

Montel: Jeff has seen, with his daughter, Q'vanaa, a need to be more patient than he needs to be with his son. More understanding, perhaps, even a little more touchy-feely. She likes to be complimented, wined and dined, and treated like a princess. Jeff's two kids are less than two years apart, and they tend to go through developmental stages at roughly the same time, but his daughter is sometimes on a completely different emotional page. She needs more hands-on attention, more loving kindness, more soft edges. Jeff has worked to understand this. He's consulted the research, but he can't find any consensus, so he relies on the anecdotal experiences of friends and patients for his fieldwork. Yes, boys and girls are different—and yes, it's sometimes okay to treat them differently. It's okay to coddle one child and be stern with another—not because you're playing favorites, but because you're playing the percentages. One child might respond better to a tough-love model, and one might respond to the soft stuff. Know your sons and daughters—know their differences, and work them to each child's advantage.

Hold High Standards for Both Sexes

Now, the flip side to this open-minded position is that there must also be a constant set of goals and ethics for all of our children—that is, the same standards. It's a negative to hold out the presidency as a career goal that's only available to your son, and a secretarial job as a goal that's only available to your daughter.

Thankfully, we're getting beyond that ice age. We're not there yet, but we're getting there, and in many fields there's no longer any "glass ceiling" through which our daughters cannot rise. But neither should we carry any different sets of expectations for the child of one gender over the child of another. If we presume that a doctor is by nature a compassionate person, and a lawyer a ruthless one, it doesn't mean that we should direct our daughters toward medicine and our sons toward the law. Let them go with their own flow. Hold our children to the same standards, no matter their gender. Teach them the same principles, the same ethics. Hope that they conduct themselves by the same code. And know that your sons and your daughters can both reach the same mountaintop, even if they reach the summit through different paths.

The interesting turnabout in this open mind-set is how to handle opposite-gender children—your daughter, if you're a dad; your son, if you're a mom. We maintain that it's not only okay for a mom to get down on the floor and wrestle with her young son, it's *necessary*—just as it's necessary for a dad to have a tea party with his daughter and her dolls. The relationship that a little girl shares with her father will imprint every male-female relationship that she has as an adult. Show her tenderness, along with firmness. Treat her like a princess, but at the same time, make sure she's not spoiled. Moms, take your sons fishing, or out to a ball game. Teach them how to act around women in traditionally female environments, and to accept women in traditionally male environments. Remember, the patterns you set early on will form their expectations as they grow up.

Female children tend to look to their fathers as barometers of whether or not they can trust men. Male children tend to look to their mothers as the foundation for the relationships they will form later in life. Keep this in mind, and set good examples. A divorced mother who constantly puts down men tells her son that he will never live up to her expectations. To her, and to other women, he will always be a disappointment.

For parents living together in the same home, pay special attention to how you treat one another, because your *children* are paying special attention to how you treat one another. You're blueprinting them for the time when they're in a committed, nurturing relationship. What you show them is what they'll know.

And, above all, celebrate what's different about each of your children. Consider the mosaic of America. We are a multicultural society, and we celebrate this fact. We were never any melting pot. That was just a headline. The real story is that we were always gonna throw everything into the soup. All the pieces are still there. It's not like a consommé. You can taste the chicken, the celery, the rice, the broth. It's all still there, and it's the same with men and women, boys and girls. We're the same, but different. Alike, but not alike. We need to actively parent our sons and our daughters to where we see them as individuals, to where they become at least somewhat independent. We know we wrote earlier not to blue-pink your newborn's brain with a seemingly color-appropriate nursery, but later on, when they can come to these choices by themselves, it's definitely okay for a girl's room to look like a girl's room, and a boy's room to look like a boy's room. Just make sure they come to this place by themselves, on their own timetables—and that you keep them company along the way.

A Father's Love

Single parents of opposite-sex children have a tougher time than we know. It's the little things that seem to fall through the cracks—but to a child, those little things loom large. Take the story of Daniel and Tricia, a father-daughter duo who came to the *Montel* show for a fashion makeover that had its roots in a very real dilemma.

How can a single father raise a young girl with enough of the feminine touches she'll need to fit in at school and feel good about herself with her peers? How can he talk to her about the changes going on in her body, the way she wears her hair, and the gender-specific ways in which little girls interact with each other . . . if he doesn't know these things for himself?

Montel and his producers were only able to help Daniel with the very surface elements of his problem, but it was a start.

Tricia was a freshman in high school, and Daniel worried that she'd become too much of a tomboy to be accepted by her peers. When she was younger, he hardly thought about these things, but now that she was a young woman, with all kinds of young-woman issues swirling around her, it sometimes seemed that he could think of little else. Her clothing was the least of it, but it was a place to start. She wore a lot of his old clothes. They were comfortable. Tricia loved her father, and loved dressing like him. "You could fit a family of five inside my pants," she kidded on the show, but the joke rankled him.

As a little girl, going into the grown-up closets to play dress-up, all she could find were men's clothing—but the gap in her influence was clearly more than cosmetic. Daniel took his daughter boating, fishing, or out to ball games, and she often accompanied him on outings with his friends. He realized that she hadn't spent enough time around women. The other kids started teasing her at school—about her clothing, at first, and soon enough about the general way in which she carried herself.

Tricia, on her end, was bruised by the teasing, but she mostly ached for her father. She hated that he had to worry about her so much, and that he felt he had failed her in this one area. He was a great father, and they had a wonderful, loving relationship, but he stayed up nights worrying about the way she couldn't quite fit in. She didn't like being teased, but she liked the way she dressed. She liked who she was. She didn't even mind her "tomboy" reputation—

although, to be honest, after she was taunted into hitting a boy in class one day, she wore the label a little differently.

As part of her on-air makeover, Tricia picked out a few comfortable dresses—nothing too frilly, but certainly feminine. The last time she had worn a dress, she said, was in church, many years earlier. She looked beautiful, with her hair done just so, but the most beautiful thing about the whole thing was how her father looked on. He was so visibly proud of her, of who she was and the choices she'd made, that it didn't much matter what she was wearing. She would have been as beautiful to him in a burlap sack as she was to Montel's viewers in a floral print.

The sweet turnabout in the duo's look was the way Tricia took the opportunity to spruce up her father's wardrobe in the bargain. She still had a weak spot for his old clothes, but she wasn't too crazy about the way they looked on him when they were ostensibly new. He tended toward khakis, with a sweater tied around his neck; and she thought the look was tired, old-fashioned, and maybe a bit too preppy. So she had him decked out in some hipper outfits, and by the time the two of them left the studio, they looked like the poster-family for a trendy clothing store.

Underneath the outward appearances, though, you could see in their relationship a willingness to work past the trouble spots in their lives, an openness to discussing anything and everything, and a closeness that beat all. Sure, it must be unthinkably tough to raise a daughter from the other side of the fence, the way a guy like Daniel's doing. Of course, a simple television makeover doesn't stretch nearly far enough to cover some of the holes in this young girl's life. And certainly, there's probably no replacing a mother's influence in the daily life of a little girl, just as there's no replacing a father's role in the daily life of a little boy.

But—and this was the great lesson of this family's example—there's also no replacing our nontraditional family dynamics when they're built on relationships that have to do with trust, caring, and effort. Sometimes it doesn't matter if you can't braid hair, or tell a child what menstrual cramps feel like, or shop for a sports bra. Sometimes the best you can do is more than enough.

◆ ◆ ◆

···CHAPTER···
SIX

PRACTICAL SCHOOLING

Let's begin this discussion with some perspective: The average starting salary for sanitation workers exceeds that of public-school teachers in virtually every region of this country. It's an abomination (in a nation that strives to be a world and technological leader) that the people who are *teaching* that technology make less money than the people who clean up the *refuse* from that technology.

Understand, we've got nothing against sanitation workers. It's a fine, respectable job—and a vitally important one at that. We applaud sanitation workers' rights to go out and earn as much money as they possibly can, because they deserve it. But we *do* have an issue with the across-the-board low salaries doled out to our nation's teachers. It's embarrassing and short-sighted, and it goes to the root of a lot of the problems confronting our children as we move headlong into this next century.

We believe that in order to maintain America's position at the head of its class, we desperately need to overhaul our education system to where the level of respect and prestige we accord our teachers is commensurate with the demands we place on the job.

We need to recruit more people of quality to the classroom. We need to hold out education as a noble and rewarding career pursuit. We need to ensure that the best and the brightest are out in front, challenging our *kids* to be the best and the brightest.

We're a long way from home on this one. In most of our communities, we spend as little as possible and hope that our teachers get the most out of our children. How can this be? Spend less, you get fewer results. Spend more, you get more results. The thinking should be that this money is not an above-the-line cost, but an investment in our shared futures.

Seniors, parents of older children, unencumbered adults . . . we don't buy the argument that you shouldn't have to pay the freight for other people's kids. Put a top-of-the-line education system in place, and we all benefit. Society benefits. Your neighborhoods are cleaner, safer, and more efficient. Your health-care and quality-of-life needs are more easily, and more intelligently, met. We're investing in our children, people, not bottom-auctioning for baby-sitting services to look after them five days a week. These are not your neighbors' issues, or the issues of the young family down the block. These are *your* issues—no matter what stage of life you're passing through. Nothing is more important.

Okay, we've had our little venting. We've said our piece. It's not our intention here to present a position paper on the state of public-school education in this country, but to help parents lay a practical foundation for the education of their children. Everything else flows from this issue right here, from the individual efforts we make with our own kids. We can rail against our misplaced societal notions regarding education until we turn blue, but the truth is that education begins at home—and in the best of all possible worlds, it should begin before your child reaches school age. And as long as we're reaching, it should be constant, and unrelenting.

You Are the Most Important Teacher

Despite all of the hours you will spend in conference with professional educators in the years ahead, never lose sight of the fact that *you* are your children's most important teacher. You are their first line of attack and their last line of defense against indifference and routine in your neighborhood schools. It starts with you, and it ends with you—and it begins the moment your child is born. Your baby's brain cells multiply at an incredible rate, especially during the first three months after birth, so the child is learning rapidly. Babies are incredibly responsive to sight, sound, smell, and motion, and they thrive on sensory stimulation, so take advantage of this opportunity—because it doesn't come around again.

Raise a child who loves to learn and you're miles ahead of the race. Be careful, though; some kids can develop a fear of learning if we push them too far too fast, or if we expect more from them than they can deliver by a certain age. If your children appear tentative about a learning activity, talk to them about it. You can probably come up with a way to help them alleviate the fear and find the fun in whatever the goal is. Sometimes children may not want to read because they have some sort of difficulty, perhaps bad vision or hearing, a learning disability, or attention deficit hyperactivity disorder (ADHD), all of which are common. Or the problems might be psychologically rooted, such as related maturation conflicts. Pay close attention to unusual behavior, and be ready to help your children work out problems. And always be ready to consult an expert for diagnosis and treatment.

As a parent, when you bring fun into the teaching equation, it can make your job a lot easier, and at the same time take away the fear of learning. If children are having fun, anxiety doesn't even come into the picture. Make rhymes for things you're trying to teach your children. Gently begin teaching them how to read, count, recite the alphabet, or do simple math. Be a working partner to your children's learning process.

Think back to when you were a child, and remember the teachers who were able to draw the most out of you. Talk to your children the way you enjoyed being spoken to: in informal, non-confrontational tones and situations—for example, during bathtime or while walking in the park. Reverse roles by allowing your kids to ask you questions, and give right and wrong answers to see if they can catch you in your "errors." Use plenty of positive verbal reinforcement.

Another practical early-parenting technique to make learning more fun is to focus on what your child can easily do. For example, together come up with words that all begin with the same letter. Make it a game, not a stressful tutoring session. Let your kids have fun, but always challenge them just a little more by taking them to the next step without expecting them to go there by themselves.

A mother we know would show her three-year-old son the word *dog* whenever it was written on the page. After a while, he started pointing out the word *dog* to her. She wouldn't have asked him to attempt such an activity unless she knew for sure that he could, because she didn't want him to feel that he had failed. If you point things out to kids, they will naturally move ahead as soon as they're ready to go there, but if you push them too soon, the effort could backfire. Know your children's limitations, and the expectations they place on themselves.

Avoid showing disappointment or frustration. Children will experience these emotions on an even larger scale than you do because they feel that they've let you down, as well as themselves. Ultimately, positive feelings will encourage learning, and negative ones will cause children to want to avoid whatever topic brought on the bad vibes. Accentuate the positive. Eliminate the negative. (Do *you* feel a song coming on, or is it just us?)

Kids develop the confidence to learn by observing proper role models—people who look like them, come from the same backgrounds, or are successful. If these role models are smart, high-achieving individuals, our kids will emulate their behavior. The problem is that many of our children are exposed to non-intellectual role models even before they begin formal education. In the black community, for example, many a kid will have a stronger desire to become an athlete or a rapper than a scholar or an educated professional. White schoolgirls would sooner be a pop star than Margaret Mead. This is a troubling phenomenon, and as parents, we should guard against it.

Positive Role Models

Self-esteem is essential to learning, and the practical parent must address this facet of their children's lives as early as possible. Seek out successful individuals (explorers, inventors, entrepreneurs) whose careers you can hold up as a model. If your child's interests are such that the role model *must* be an athlete, make sure it's an educated, civic-minded athlete who presents a positive ideal. Indeed, sometimes the best role-modeling is closer at hand than you realize, and your kids won't have to go looking at athletes or models or movie stars. Cast yourselves as role models, and instill in your children a practical pattern they might follow. Provide love and nurturing to build self-esteem and the confidence to learn.

To be a better role model at home, work to maintain a stable family life, and avoid fighting with your spouse. Instead, discuss issues in a calm manner, and don't lose your temper. If you have a hot-headed nature, this type of patterning will keep you from "going off" on strangers in public places, and possibly prevent you from calling your own child "stupid" or "dumb." Even if it's unintentional, name-calling can be one of the most damaging things a parent can do, and showing irrational anger toward strangers can also set a dangerous model. Quietly work out your spousal disagreements, and make sure never to denigrate your child's intelligence. People of average and even below-average intelligence with above-average doses of self-esteem and confidence can achieve more in life than geniuses who lack these qualities.

Believe in yourself and your own abilities. If needed, consider therapy or any number of winning self-help and motivational books to bolster your own sense of self. If you believe in yourself, that confidence will be communicated to your children, who will in turn feel good about themselves.

Set a good example by being involved in educational pursuits. Take night courses (or correspondence courses) in topics that you're interested in. Turn that equivalency diploma into the real deal, or finish that undergraduate degree that you almost got before you quit to get married. Start on a master's degree. And realize that your pursuit does not have to be academic—even a carpentry or cooking course will prove rewarding, and set a positive pattern for your child to follow. Through your actions and initiatives, your child will begin to see the pursuit of education and learning as an expected and normal part of life.

Additional Stimulation

Yes, education *does* begin at home, but many people let their children get too much of that "education" from television—what we call the "baby-sitter in a box." Chronic television viewing encourages passivity, which is not desirable for active learning. You want your children to be participants in education, not just members of an audience. Nielsen audience rating studies show that kids typically watch more than two hours of television each day, yet they do only one hour of homework or independent reading. Restrict *how much* they watch, and control *what* they watch. For preschool kids, the rule of thumb should be no more than one hour a day of cartoons, or maybe a family-oriented sitcom that imparts good values. If they want to watch more television, instead of cartoons or sitcoms have them watch educational programming such as *Sesame Street, Reading Rainbow, The Magic School Bus,* or *Blue's Clues*—all on PBS. (The Disney

Channel and Nickelodeon also offer some excellent educational programming options.) By the way, *Sesame Street* features an excellent blend of characters and images from all races that are portrayed as equals.

You must be strong here, because kids will cajole, scream, and blackmail to get more time in front of the tube. If you establish control over what they watch early on, you'll be better off. Good habits are easy to start, and bad ones are hard to break. Instead of letting television executives program your family's viewing, take matters into your own hands and use the local library as a resource for family-oriented movies, documentaries, and educational fare.

Use television to your advantage. Supplement some of your own programming choices with appropriate reading. If your family plans to watch a network mini-series inspired by *Gulliver's Travels,* seek out the book on which it was based. You'll find abridged or updated versions appropriate to every reading level— and the complete, unabridged text for older kids.

And speaking of reading, the best way to get your children on the path to a good education is to read to them as *early* and as *often* as possible. Kids have vivid imaginations, and they always enjoy hearing stories and then later reading them. Make the purchase of a book an event. Take them to the children's book section and let them see the array of materials. Thumb through several to stimulate their interest, and then steer them toward the purchase of a title that imparts good values and sparks their creative thinking. Local libraries often have group readings for children and feature guest authors. Call your library and get on the mailing list of events. Visit the library at least once a week with your children. As they get older, teach them how to navigate their way around the reference section—where they will eventually do research for projects and term papers. The magazine rack is also a good resource for children of all ages.

Naturally, this active search for stimulation doesn't end with reading. Your home should be filled not only with books, but with toys and games that occupy your child's mind and body. If you haven't already done so, consider investing in a computer. There are several models from leading manufacturers that are priced at family-friendly levels (less than $1,000 for a complete setup, including printer). One recent study found that children who began "playing" with home computers at an early age developed higher IQs than those who had no access to a computer.

Games are also essential, although here we look away from most of the mindless video games that have permeated our culture over the past several years. Sure, there's research to suggest that these games develop important hand-eye coordination functioning, but we don't buy it as an excuse to waste time in front of a video screen. We'd rather see our kids playing board games and interacting with each other in simpler, more creative activities. "Candyland" is fun and teaches children colors and the rudiments of board-game playing. "Trouble" teaches counting. "Monopoly, Jr." is good for math skills. "Connect/Four" helps with sequential and abstract thinking.

Encourage children to live up to their potential. Make sure that their games teach them new concepts and lead to greater learning skills. Products such as science kits, puzzles, and creative toys like those that encourage building and art will bring out wonderful talents.

You can work with your children to decorate their room to reflect their interests. Letting your children use their room as a means of self-expression is a wonderful confidence builder and will develop creativity. They will want to put up their own artwork and posters representing things they like. You can make a game out of clipping pictures from magazines of all the people, animals, cars, colors, and other things that turn them on. Make this into a collage, which can be supplemented regularly. This is also a good way to get to know your children better, to see what triggers their positive or negative responses.

Next, expose your kids in a nonthreatening way to highly stimulating pursuits such as music or the arts—especially if they show some hint of innate ability at an early age. Toy musical instruments sometimes bring out natural talents in young children. Most children will be able to extract some sort of tuneful noise out of a recorder or kiddie guitar, but exceptional kids will produce a more disciplined sound. If you play an instrument, let them see you having fun playing it. Teach them a simple tune, such as "Three Blind Mice" or "Chopsticks." If you want them to learn a musical instrument such as the piano, pay for a few lessons to see how they respond. Make sure the instructor is "child-friendly" and upbeat—leave the humorless disciplinarians to others. You might even consider taking a few lessons yourself in order to be a role model for your child. You can practice together and play together.

Studies have shown that children who learn to read music and who know how to play a musical instrument present higher science and math scores in school throughout their academic careers. They also learn to employ better abstract and spatial reasoning.

To encourage music appreciation, leave a radio on at appropriate times. Classical music may not suit everyone's taste, and may seem highbrow or uppity, but there are times when the music of Bach or Chopin, for example, seems to add sanity to a chaotic world.

Montel: As a jazz musician, Jeff wanted his children to enjoy jazz, so he kept his dial tuned to a local jazz station and hoped something might rub off.

Some children show early signs of being natural artists and should be encouraged accordingly. Keep plenty of art supplies handy. Once the budding artist has mastered the medium of crayons, give him or her a gift box of colored pencils, artist's brushes, inks, and special paper.

Developing Proper Educational Habits

And yet despite all of these creative initiatives in the home, our children will be left to their own devices once they start school—and here we need to shift our focus from primary educator to watchdog. Many of our kids develop bad habits when it comes to education. They don't do their homework, or they hand in sloppy and incomplete assignments.

Montel: In Jeff's family therapy practice, he has lately seen an epidemic of children who fail multiple classes. Remember when failing even *one* class was not acceptable? Oh, how times have changed!

What makes this situation even sadder is that these kids have no idea that they're destroying their futures. Education has lost all importance to them. They really think that there are no consequences for failing grades. They don't seem to understand that failing grades in high school, even in the freshman year, will drastically reduce their chances of getting into a decent college—or, for that matter, *any* college at all. You're either college-bound or you're not, and this will determine the path of your life.

Let your children know that their failing grades will not be tolerated, and impress upon them that their future is at stake. At the same time, make it clear that you're willing to listen to whatever problem is causing the poor academic performance. If you believe that your son is failing in school due to low self-esteem, address the causes immediately. If your daughter doesn't believe in herself, or is insecure about some aspect of her appearance, talk about it and listen as much as possible. If she needs you to be a "cheerleader" to provide encouragement, then do it.

Never allow your children to skip school just because they're too tired or don't feel like going. Giving in will make the problem worse. Your children will curiously start "getting tired" the morning of tests and quizzes. In extreme cases, skipping school can erode self-discipline in other aspects of life. If your children currently have problems with truancy, get to work on it right away with their teacher. Suggest that your children bring home a signed attendance slip every day until you can reestablish the trust you'll need to set this problem aside. Initiate a heart-to-heart talk with your kids (it usually takes more than one!), to discuss what is keeping them away from classes or school. Then address each issue with problem-solving behaviors. Talk to other parents to see how they've dealt with these issues.

Help your children set schedules for homework and study. Self-discipline is the most effective method of maintaining confidence, success, and interest in school. If your children are beginning to have problems in the classroom, a disorganized personality will further contribute to academic problems. Sit down with your kids and jointly work out a simple daily schedule that organizes the tasks ahead. Make sure that your children are actively involved in creating this schedule. If they follow the schedule, reward them at the end of the week with something simple, like pizza, a video, or a CD. These things might seem like extortion, or direct payment, but these "incentive programs" work until self-induced enlightenment sets in!

Make homework a top priority in your household. It's very important that it be the children's first activity upon coming home from school. Getting it done gets it out of the way, promotes efficiency in the long run, and reduces anxiety. Going out to play or hanging out with friends should always be contingent upon the completion of schoolwork. Don't be swayed by your children's excuses, crocodile tears, or promises that it will be done later. This is a time when you need to be rigid and consistent. You must convey that you mean business.

Make it known to your kids that education is the most important value that they must incorporate into their lives. This means constantly discussing the importance of school as the foundation for any type of success in life. As soon as your children understand speech, begin to talk about the importance of learning and school. As your kids get older, discuss the merits of college and professional schools. Be sure to present this as a goal, not an option. Try to be a role model yourself. If *you* went to college, talk about your education. If you didn't attend, talk about what you've missed—and how you'd like to have some of it back. If your kids see you working hard to improve yourself, they'll most likely follow your example.

For athletic children, it's okay to discuss college in terms of where they might pursue their sport and their education at the same time. The two are not mutually exclusive; on the contrary, scholastics and athletics complement each other. (Healthy body, healthy mind!)

Become involved in your school district. Find the time to attend school board meetings. Let your voice be heard as a school volunteer or member of the PTA or city council. Hold your elected officials accountable for any educational budget cuts. Call. Write. E-mail. Fax. Make yourself a complete pain-in-the-butt. Remember, these people work for you. They represent your interests, so let them start representing.

If you know of incompetent teachers or corrupt administrators, make sure that their actions are brought to the attention of authorities. A scandal recently broke out in Staten Island, New York, where school administrators were admitting children to a magnet school based on political connections rather than merit. Evidently, the children of public officials and friends of the school staff were being placed ahead of children who legitimately scored well on the entrance exams. It took the courage of one parent to bring this unfair situation to light. Regrettably, this was not an isolated incident. School boards are being replaced all the time due to wrongdoing and unethical practices.

Be a partner to your children's teachers. Let them know that you're totally invested in your kids' education. Stay in frequent contact so that you know how your children are doing. Visit the classroom at least once a month. Teachers need to know that you care and are following up at home; it will motivate them to work harder with your children.

Special Needs, Special Challenges

If your children are receiving any type of special education, this advice is doubly important. Special education programs are usually poorly funded and inadequately staffed. Many are merely baby-sitting centers for children who are unable to function in regular classrooms. For example, children with severe acting-out behaviors are mixed with children who have other types of disabilities, such as learning disorders. The classrooms are often noisy and unstructured and not conducive to any real teaching. Too often, we see children with behavior problems cast as pariahs in the educational system. Kids who act out (which can mean they're disruptive, talk out of turn, or are unable to focus) are immediately labeled as troublemakers, and rarely does anyone bother to look at the possible root causes of their behavior. Additional funding might mitigate the problem, providing teachers and other school personnel with more training on how to better understand, counsel, and manage students exhibiting acting-out behaviors.

The key for parents of special-ed students is to find out what the school's resources and procedures are, and the prognosis and options for your children. Certain behaviors are routinely misdiagnosed as anti-social personality or conduct disorders, resulting in improper treatment and continued failure in the classroom. Quite often, behavioral problems are not related to emotional issues or instability. Instead, they may be symptoms related to dyslexia, learning disabilities, or even ADHD. *Dyslexia,* for those new to the term, is a neurological disorder in which numbers and/or letters are mentally processed and perceived in an inverted manner, resulting in reading, mathematical, reasoning, communication, and memory problems.

Learning disabilities describe any in a series of physiological (psychological and physical) disorders that also interfere with reading, mathematics, or written expression. *Attention deficit hyperactivity disorder (ADHD)* is a physiological disorder causing a persistent pattern of inattention and/or hyperactivity and impulsiveness that usually presents itself before the age of seven. All three of these disorders make it nearly impossible for children to keep up in class. Because children can't understand why they don't seem able to learn, they will often feel stupid and demoralized, develop low self-esteem, and show a deficit in social skills. The result is a child who is frustrated and therefore acts out angrily in class and at home.

Montel: In his practice, Jeff has seen many children who have been on Ritalin (the prescription medication of choice for the treatment of ADHD kids) without accompanying therapy. Many parents are simply not informed enough to know the proper treatment for ADHD, and they accept the recommendations of the school without question. In most cases, there should be a three-step program of behavior modification, psychotherapy, and (if needed) medication.

We can't stress enough that medication should only be used as a last resort. Behavioral therapies should be tried first. If your children are taking medication to control their behavior, they should be monitored for side effects, which may include sleeplessness and poor appetite. Try to keep the dosage prescribed by the psychiatrist to the minimum effective amount. Finally, always have your child's liver functioning monitored every few weeks to see how well it's metabolizing the drug. Your doctor should tell you all of this, but sometimes even the most diligent professionals get distracted, so take the initiative.

As practical parents, we cannot trust others with the future of our children. We can't trust our communities to make appropriate decisions regarding teacher salaries, and we can't trust our teachers to make appropriate diagnoses regarding our kids' behavior. Absolutely, it *does* take a village to raise a child, but even more important, it takes a parent (yes, one will suffice!) to be the primary caretaker, advocate, and leader in a child's educational life. From the moment you take your children home from the hospital to the moment they earn their college degrees, it falls to you. And know this: Not a single one of the practical-parenting strategies set forth in this chapter will help your children if you do not also let them know that you love them and believe in their abilities to succeed in school. They won't get that support from their peers, from their communities, or from their teachers, so *you* have to provide it. Remember, it starts with *you*, and it ends with *you*.

And so, as our kids are fond of saying, "Gas 'em up, gas 'em up, gas 'em up!"

Practicing What You Preach

Patricia, a 49-year-old single mother and dress shop owner, had trouble getting her 13-year-old daughter, Nancy, to understand the value of school and education. Patricia's business was successful beyond her most realistic dreams, and she thought she was presenting a positive pattern for her daughter to follow, but Nancy and school just didn't get along, to the point that where the issue had become the focus of pretty much all of the tension in their household.

They reached out to Jeff for family counseling, and together discovered that positive role modeling doesn't always do the job on its own. See, Nancy was a below-average student. School didn't come easily for her, but more than that, her interests ran toward MTV and hanging out with her girlfriends. She didn't see any reason to push herself in school—especially considering the fact that her mother had managed to make something of herself without any higher education. Whenever Patricia pushed her daughter to spend more time on her studies, Nancy became confrontational, and it was during one of the resulting standoffs that the two of them went to see Jeff.

It came out in therapy that because Patricia had never attended college but had somehow built a successful small business, a confusing mixed message was picked up by her daughter. It suggested that there was no reason to work hard in school because you can achieve your goals later in life without a traditional foundation, and it also reminded Nancy that education had not been a priority for her mother when she was young. It was one of those "do-as-I-say-not-as-I-do" situations.

All along, Patricia had thought she was setting a good example through hard work and persistence, but what she saw as resourcefulness, and capitalizing on her second chances, her daughter saw as a ready excuse to put off until tomorrow what she had no interest in today.

Ultimately, Patricia realized that if Nancy was ever going to take her arguments on the importance of education at least halfway seriously, she would have to walk the walk as well as talk the talk, so she went back to school herself. It wasn't enough to succeed in business. It wasn't enough to create an environment in the home that celebrated learning. To get the message home to her child that school was important, Patricia decided to finally get her degree. She started taking part-time college courses. Happily, Nancy realized that her mother wasn't all talk, and she soon became more serious about her own schoolwork and academic goals. The two even found time to study together, rewarding themselves for their hard work with a shared dish of ice cream or a favorite television show.

Too often, we find, parents make a lot of noise about hard work and diligence, yet their own lives run completely counter to their advice. Frequently, it's because they never had an opportunity for the kind of education they're now in a position to afford for their children. Other times, it's because they came to this realization too late for themselves, and they're simply making sure their children don't repeat their mistakes. Nancy never came out and pointed a finger at her mother, and it's possible that she never understood her mom's feelings on the importance of education, but once they were raised in this light, and once Patricia responded by going back to school, it made all the difference.

◆ ◆ ◆

···CHAPTER···
SEVEN

PRACTICAL MONITORING

O ne of the greatest concerns confronting contemporary parents is how to shield their children from all sorts of negative external influences. Television. Music. Fashion. The World Wide Web. A complacent teacher. An absent-minded parent of a friend. Our kids are assaulted by so many outside impulses and images that it's a wonder their little heads don't explode.

But do you know what? They don't. They can handle pretty much everything the arbiters of pop-cultural cool can throw at them (and probably a little bit more, besides), and they're usually a better judge of character than we acknowledge. Give them credit. Kids, for the most part, know where to put these constant shifts in taste, style, and status, and they can usually discern between appropriate and inappropriate behavior. They know the basic difference between right and wrong, even if they sometimes get tripped up on the shading.

It's the parents who seem to have trouble dealing with things, so we're here to tell you that we don't count ourselves among those who look to shut out these external influences, or keep our kids closeted from the confusing batch of mixed messages that define our cultural identities. That, we maintain, would be counterproductive, short-sighted, and more than a little like the parents we vowed never to become. Instead, we embrace these influences—and somewhere in the shift we believe we're better equipped to help our children process this barrage of external information.

Montel: Jeff tells his patients all the time to tackle these influences head-on. After all, he reasons, you can't censor what your children hear or troubleshoot their relationships any more than you can reshape their beliefs, but you better be out there on the front lines, monitoring what they take in, checking things out for yourself. Learn what makes your kids tick and hum. Connect with your children through their interests, and they will no longer stand as impediments to success, but stepping-stones to a vibrant, shared future.

With our smallest children, watchdogging is most important. Books, games, videos, computer programs, and certain kid-friendly Internet sites should all play a role in early child development, and parents must absolutely hold a firm hand in helping to shape that role. But what most young parents fail to realize is that the greatest external influence in the life of a young child of working parents is the baby-sitter, or the designated caregiver who looks after the kid during the workday. It doesn't matter if it's a grandparent, a neighbor, an in-home nanny, or a licensed child-care provider. That individual, or group of individuals, will probably play a larger developmental impact on your child than anyone but you—and because they are *anyone but you*, we categorize them as an external influence. The same holds true for your older children's teachers, and we'll get to them in the pages ahead.

External Influences

Look, we've all worked for a living, in one form or another, or at one time or another. We know what it's like to punch a clock and log long hours on someone else's agenda, and what it's like for that work to matter more to someone else than it does to you. How many of us can truly say we gave 100 percent of ourselves every time we showed up for work? Even the best workers have a bad day—and even on a good day, they don't work at full throttle, all the time. So why would we think that an individual paid to look after our children is any different? Maybe they're attentive 75 percent of the time (and that's probably a high-end estimate!). Maybe they become irritable at the end of the day. Maybe they find themselves wishing they were somewhere else—taking care of their own children, perhaps.

They don't mean to bring a negative influence into the equation, but there it is. They don't smile enough. They don't interact enough. They don't communicate enough. They don't educate enough. So, yeah, as early as day care and preschool, you've got to be on top of whoever it is that comes into contact with your children. Check these people out. Don't expect the world, and know that at certain times during the day, they won't be fully available to your children, so plan accordingly. Maybe you'll have to overcompensate a bit when you first reconnect with your kids at the end of the day to make up for those times when they may have been left to cry a beat or two too long, or when a thought they'd wanted to articulate went unexpressed because there was no one around who seemed to want to hear it.

Another area parents tend to overlook are the friends our young children make—in day care, on the playground, or in preschool. Here, too, the emphasis should be on practical pairings that benefit each child, and not on convenient "play-dates" arranged by baby-sitters who happen to be friendly. In many communities, the mad rush to schedule activities for small children has left our kids with a stunning inability to amuse themselves, to negotiate external relationships on their own, or to develop friendships of their choosing. The world has changed, somewhat, from when we were kids, and a certain amount of this programmed interaction is in response to some of the more insidious external influences in our communities, but let's not go overboard. Let's remember that our kids are kids.

As parents, we both tried to re-create for our children something of the spontaneity we enjoyed as kids. However, living a public life, as Montel does; and a New York City lifestyle, as Jeff does, made this somewhat difficult. Still, we found ways to manage, and whatever your circumstances, you can, too. Create a safe environment in your neighborhood where your small children can move about in relative freedom. Supervise from a distance—but *do* supervise, while at the same time encouraging your children to interact as social animals while making some of their own choices.

Discover opportunities to teach self-reliance, even as you roam the sidelines, monitoring the scene. And try to dissuade your kids from associating with playmates who are not a good match for them. A child with older siblings, for example, may use inappropriate language or act like a bully, and it makes no sense to schedule activities with this child just because the parents or babysitters are friendly. An only child of toddler age might have trouble sharing his or her toys, and you might feel uncomfortable having your child suffer the toddler's slings and arrows while this kid learns how to cooperate. Let your children determine who they want to spend time with, and on what terms.

Good Teachers Are Crucial

Now, on to the most powerfully influential individuals who will be in daily contact with your child. Never assume that every teacher is a good teacher. They might be trained professionals, but as in any profession, some are more professional than others.

We've heard hundreds of stories of otherwise valued teachers pre-judging students based on the color of their skin, their economic status, or their family situation at home. They'll say things such as, "That's okay, Timmy, you probably don't know how to do this, but let me show you." And meanwhile, Timmy's sitting there at his desk thinking, *Maybe I do and maybe I don't, but let me try. Let me let you down.* Teach your children to define who they are and what they might accomplish—and if you do it right, no lazy, judgmental teacher will ever get in his way.

Jeff: When Montel was eight years old, he had a negative encounter with his third-grade teacher that resonates to this day. He wrote about this situation in his book *Mountain, Get Out of My Way,* and regards it as one of the defining moments of his life. Here's what happened. Montel had written a Christmas story about some of the presents he needed to wrap, and he made an entirely innocent spelling mistake. Instead of "wrapped," he wrote "raped," and the teacher circled the word in red and placed a big old "F" on his paper. He was devastated. He'd always gotten the highest marks on his papers and tests, and he had no idea what was wrong with this effort, so he approached the teacher after class and asked if maybe there had been some sort of mistake. She grabbed the paper from his hand, took a quick glance at it, and then shot Montel a look that could have chilled tea. "That's the reason why you people will never be nothin' in life," she said, unpleasantly. "You only have one thing on your mind."

That was all this *professional* had to say on the matter, and Montel ran home in shame and hid the paper from his parents. He didn't know what he'd done to set this woman off, but figured it must have been pretty bad, and he wasn't about to get chewed out at home for it as well. Years later, when he learned how to use a dictionary, Montel finally figured out what had rubbed this narrow-minded woman the wrong way. He looked up the word *raped,* and he realized the confusion, but he still couldn't accept the condemnation. He couldn't accept that by the phrase "you people" she had meant "you black people." He couldn't accept that this was how he'd been treated. To this day, he regards that third-grade teacher as the first true mountain in his path, and he feels certain that if he hadn't bumped into her when he did, his life might have taken another road.

So this story is told here as a cautionary device. Ignorance is all around, and it can't help but find your children sooner or later. They'll encounter ignorant day-care providers, ignorant teachers, ignorant bosses, ignorant neighbors. And you'll have to help them deal with it. You can teach your kids to rise above the ignorance of others, as Montel was able to do with that teacher of his, or they can shrink in the face of it.

Whatever you do, learn as much as you can about the people who will be close to your children on a daily basis, especially to your preschool kids, who might not be able to fully express their feelings about how things are going. As they get older, your children will be better able to share with you the nature of all of their adult-child relationships, and their peer-group friendships as well.

Listen and Learn

As our children grow, so, too, does the world around them—and if we've had our own heads in the sand a little bit, culturally speaking, this is where we need to pick them up and take a look around. We'd hate like hell to be like some of those clueless parents we remember from our own childhoods—you know, those plaid-pants-wearing, Perry Como-listening dads you see parodied on *Saturday Night Live*. No way was that ever gonna be either one of us. And, we're guessing, you're not quick to claim the stereotype for yourselves, either, so the time has come to put a couple hip-hop and top-40 stations on your car radio's preprogrammed dial; and to start checking out MTV, VH-1, BET, and Nickelodeon on television. You'll probably also want to log on to some of the more popular teen-oriented Websites to determine the kind of material that reaches your kids electronically, and thumb through some of the magazines that may have started coming into your house through the mail.

There's a whole lot out there—you don't need us to tell you that—but perhaps you *do* need a push to get as familiar with as much of the stuff as you possibly can. Back when *we* were kids, we pretty much moved about in a vacuum, and we liked to think that our parents had no idea what was going on. Indeed, that was very often the case, but the world has changed. There's violence in our schools, derogatory references to women on our radios, and soft-corn pornography in our PG-13 movies. Naturally, you can't shut your kids off from every TV show that comes into your home, or every movie that comes to your neighborhood multiplex—and you certainly can't screen everything before you let your child take it in. Who's got the time?

The trick, we've determined, is to take every one of these potential negatives and turn them into a positive experience. Watch questionable material with your children, and use it as a basis for a trust-building conversation. We're not suggesting that you go out and rent *Behind the Green Door* for an evening of questionable family viewing. (And the fact that we mentioned *Behind the Green Door* shows you how out-of-it we parents must sometimes seem, because surely that's become one of the tamest adult videos on the market, judging by today's standards.) No, we're simply advocating an open-minded policy that allows you and your children to explore new areas together.

Don't be judgmental. Offer your opinion, but respect your child's opinion as well. There's no right or wrong here, but you *can* and *should* set the limits in your own home. If you find a CD or video too offensive, or otherwise objectionable, then by all means . . . object. But know this: What *you* can censor, *they* can find. What you *hide*, they will *seek*. Sure, keep it out of the house if there are younger children around. And yes, keep it out of the house if it runs so counter to the ethics you're otherwise trying to instill that to allow it would seem like an endorsement of some kind. There's no reason why your two-year-old has to be quoting Adam Sandler or Chris Rock, and there's no reason why you have to be exposed to negative or explicit material either, but your ten-year-old is gonna find these things whether you let them into your house or not. More likely, they'll find *your child*—that's the power of our various media these days. The Powers That Be have got our kids wired to where it sometimes seems as if it's the kids being programmed instead of the other way around.

Listen to your kids' music. Really listen. The music industry (and here we include music videos) has undoubtedly had as much influence on the style and attitude of our young people as any other outside source. Kids four and five years old can spot Britney Spears in a line-up, or tell you the names of all the Backstreet Boys, or recite the lyrics to Kid Rock's latest single. Youth culture can't be just catalogued as hip-hop or street or mainstream. It's everything—all at once and rolled together. Listen to the lyrics of a popular rap song and you'll probably cringe, but then ask some kids to repeat them for you. Chances are, they won't be able to, at least not without the underlying beat. Studies have shown that a majority of younger kids have committed these sometimes hateful lyrics to the part of their brain that allows them to mimic in syncopation with the music, but they can't tell you later what it is they've just said. They have no idea.

We're not sure whether this is a good or a bad thing, but it's how it is—for many kids. For others, though, the lyrics to a lot of these songs are profoundly disturbing, and this is where parents need to be on their guard.

Jeff: There's a new one from Eminem that basically permeates Montel's household—and he's thinking that there's not much he can do but wait until it goes away. That, and use it as a starting-off point for a discussion with his two older daughters.

"What do you think it means when he says, 'Dunk that chick'? Or, 'Hit her at home base'?"

I don't know. Maybe he's talking about intercourse.

"Probably, but do you think that's the way sex should be between two people? Do you think that's how the guy should talk about it?"

Not really, no. Not when you put it that way.

The lyrics tell us a lot about our kids on a societal level—after all, most of these songs are written by young people not too terribly far removed from high school—but they also tell us a lot about our own kids, on an individual level. The lyrics strike some sort of chord, and we need to get at that chord if we mean to understand what's driving our children, what's holding their interest. It's one thing to suggest that rap and hip-hop denigrates women, really degrades them to this sort of base, animal-instinct level, but then when we hear our teenage daughters dismiss the words as a caricature, or a put-down aimed at men who do disregard women in this way, it's something else entirely. Listen to the words, but read between the lines—and pay attention to how the whole package is filtering through.

The images tell us a whole lot more, and here, too, we should look at them as talking points, as teaching opportunities.

"Why is every girl in these videos half-naked?"

They're hot. They're unashamed to go after what they want.

"Is that it? Are you sure?"

Maybe they want the guy to notice her.

"He's got to see the whole package before he can even say, 'Man, I think she's attractive.' Does that make any sense?"

Well, when you put it that way . . .

Kids, for the most part, get it; parents, for the most part, don't. But the practical parent is the one who will make every effort to interpret these influences from every possible angle. Every song, every video, and every R-rated movie deserves a chance, no matter how hateful or derogatory the material seems on its face, because our kids deserve a chance, and each piece has something to teach us about what's important in our child's world.

Seek opportunities for related discussions. Each day, it seems, there's a hip-hop, pop, or rap artist making dubious headlines. It's often a good idea to clip articles and share them with your kids, helping to spur a dialogue. Watch the news together and see what turns up. Something always does. For example, when the artist L'il Kim was banned from staging a New Jersey concert after authorities noticed that her celebrated X-rated, hip-hop and rap shows began at midnight, violating state cabaret and building-code regulations, it offered local parents a perfect opportunity to connect their kids' interests to the interests of the community.

When L'il Kim ignored the ban and held the concert anyway, she sent an obvious message of defiance, which in turn presented another clear line of discussion. The related news coverage was front-loaded with topics worthy of parent-child exploration: What are some other, more law-abiding ways to make your point? How important is it to hold your position and fight for what you think is right? Was there racism behind the authorities' attempt to ban the concert? What are some of the mixed messages behind L'il Kim's racy image, and is it possible that these contributed to a knee-jerk reaction against her performance?

Consider, for a moment, how the world has changed in the last couple of generations. A lot of what passes for mainstream entertainment today would have been sold as black-market erotica just 30 years ago. (Hell, even the posters on the sides of city buses would have once been viewed by adolescent boys, under the covers, with a flashlight.) The way the *average* teenage girl dresses would have cast her as a tramp. The way the *average* teenage boy has adopted the jailhouse, gang attire of the inner city would have sent social psychologists reeling. The way upper-middle-class kids drop a hundred bucks on dinner and a movie, talk endlessly to each other on their cell phones, and tool around in suped-up, stylin' vehicles . . . well, let's just say the world has changed, and we've got to change along with it. We've got to get along, *to get along.*

The easy comparison to this cultural shift is how teenage girls reacted to the Beatles back in the early 1960s. They screamed. They swooned. They cried. If one of the Fab Four even flashed a smile in their fans' direction, these girls probably would have fainted. Contrast that to how a teenage girl today reacts to the Backstreet Boys or 'N Sync. She slinks her way to the front row and shouts, "Pick me!" or sends her number backstage with an alluring message. At 15 years old!

So, yeah, listen to what they're listening to. Watch what they're watching. Get involved in their education, in who their friends are, in what they're thinking about. In the end, that's what our kids really want. They want to grow and flourish, but they want to keep connected to their parents, to their homes, to their families. That's the baseline. They'll stray a little, and they'll experiment a little, but they want to know what the boundaries are.

You, the practical parent, help them draw those lines.

Taking Care

Sometimes a parent does such a remarkable job of preparing a child for a worst-case scenario that the child is able to take even the unimaginable in stride. Consider the remarkable story of a nine-year-old boy named Travis, who appeared on the *Montel* show in late 1999. Travis's story—shocking and extreme on its face—is testimony to the strong will of our youngest children, and the ability of some to follow through on their parents' advice when everything around them is chaos and uncertainty.

On the evening of November 3, 1999, Travis's mother, Crystal, was preparing dinner in the small kitchen of their Memphis home. Crystal was a single mother. Travis was conceived during a brief affair his mother had while she was in the army, and Travis's father was never a part of his life. Money was tight, but by all accounts, Crystal was a positive role model and a good mother. She did what she could. She and her son were extremely close, and she taught Travis to be independent, instilling in him a sense of discipline and a kind of us-against-the-world mind-set that she felt would serve him well. It was the way that she saw the world, and the way she felt the world looked back on the two of them. On top of all that, she suffered from a heart ailment and worried what might become of Travis if she died.

Travis was playing in another room when he heard a loud noise. He ran into the kitchen and saw his mother on the floor. He ran to the telephone to dial 911, as he'd been taught, but the phone was dead. His mother had been unable to pay the last few bills, and service had been cut off. That was how things were in Travis's house. They sometimes had to do without telephone service, but there was always enough to eat, and decent clothes to wear. He put down the phone and went back to check on his mother. He could tell she wasn't breathing. They'd talked about this in very specific terms. He didn't panic, and kicked into action his mother's plan—in a literal sense she had never intended.

Crystal had wanted Travis to be able to take care of himself once she was gone. She wanted him to be able to manage money, prepare his own food, take out the garbage, and keep himself safe. She meant to be here for him, but she knew this would not always be possible, and when she died, Travis took her teaching on its face. He covered his mother's body with a blanket and went about his business. He was not an immoral child. He was distraught over his mother's death, but at the same time he was so terrified of being sent off to live in a foster home with strangers that he couldn't bring himself to tell anyone what had happened to his mother. He missed her terribly, wanted desperately to do the right thing, what his mother always expected of him, and this was what his nine-year-old head came up with.

For the next month, Travis bathed himself, washed his clothes, and shopped for food. He cleaned the house, did the dishes, and took out the trash. He even arranged for a money order and paid the electric bill, using some of the cash his mother had set aside. He did not miss one day of school or a single homework assignment. When the school bus driver told him that his hair was getting a little too long, Travis went home and cut it himself.

Finally, after 33 days, a family friend discovered the truth. Travis was devastated. He begged the woman not to tell anyone his secret. He insisted he would be okay. The woman had no choice but to tell the authorities—she couldn't immediately take him into her own home, because she was not family—and she can still remember Travis's panicked face, looking back at her from the rear window of the squad car as he was taken into custody. As upset as he was about his mother's death, he was even more terrified of the prospect of foster care. He had friends in school who had been shuffled so often from one home to the next, and he'd heard so many horror stories about their experiences, that he had the whole scene built up in his mind to where it was unimaginable.

Travis's story is truly an incredible tale of one boy's resolve to take care of himself despite his harrowing circumstances. We share it here not for the sensational "tabloid" aspects of the case, but for the way it compellingly illustrates how much influence a practical parent can truly have on a child—even if that influence is carried out, as it arguably was in this case, in an impractical way. Never underestimate the power of a parent's patience or love, or the power of a small child to overcome the greatest obstacles and fall back on what he's learned at home. Teach your children well, accommodate their concerns, and they will walk the path you've laid out together.

···CHAPTER··· EIGHT

PRACTICAL PRECAUTION

W e hate to have to tackle this tough issue, but we live in a world where there's no looking away from it. The sexual abuse of our young children has reached epidemic proportions, and no book on practical parenting would be complete without a careful consideration of this disturbing fact of family life—and an exploration of some of the reasonable measures you might take to protect your children.

Keeping Your Children Safe

If you're like us, you probably long for the time when it was safe to send your adolescent child alone on a bicycle ride around the block, when nursery school safety programs weren't so all-encompassing that your kid didn't come home worried about "stranger danger," and when the relative safety of your neighborhood wasn't processed in such violent terms. But that time has passed, and today's parents really need to take a practical approach to the shift in our cultural paradigm.

The reasons for the shift are apparent everywhere. These days, many parents must work both a full- and a part-time job in order to make ends meet, which translates into less time spent directly caring for their children, and trusting others to do so. Sometimes relatives or grandparents are available to help out, but most often, parents end up utilizing baby-sitters and day-care centers to fill in the gaps. Now, there's nothing wrong with seeking help in caring for your children, at least not on a case-by-case basis, but on the societal level, we have to expect a real impact.

The Children's Defense Fund reports that there are 13 million preschoolers (including 6 million infants and toddlers) spending all or some of their day being cared for by someone other than their parents. Regrettably, some of these sitters and day-care centers are unlicensed and of poor quality. Because of the lack of regulatory controls, these sitters and workers are not properly screened by any licensing agencies, which means that the chances of our kids being exposed to molesters in child-care settings is greatly increased. Granted, child sexual abuse can happen in licensed establishments, and that's also a big worry, but our children are obviously at a greater risk in unlicensed settings. And it's not just the caregivers who give us cause for concern; the lack of proper supervision in some of these group settings also allows for children with emotional problems to molest our kids.

Study after study tells us that most sexual abuse, especially when perpetrated by adults against children, involves alcohol or drugs, at least to some degree. These chemicals lower inhibition, resulting in the emergence of inappropriate behaviors, which are manifestations of internal conflicts. In other words, really screwed-up people are not able to control themselves when they're drinking or drugging. Wherever alcohol and drug abuse is widespread, for example, accompanying cases of sexual abuse also occur in large numbers.

And yet despite race or culture, sexual predators are all around us. They come in all sizes, shapes, and colors. They can be strangers, neighbors, teachers, siblings, parents, or family friends. Note, however, that men abuse children with greater frequency than women, with 95 percent of sexual abuse of girls and 80 percent of sexual abuse of boys committed by men. Although girls are more likely to be abused, boys are also vulnerable. A new study conducted by Louis Harris and Associates found that one in eight high school boys had been physically or sexually abused. Among those who were sexually abused, about one-third reported that the abuse happened at home, and 45 percent said the abuser was a family member.

It's gotten to the point where nothing is sacred, as even pillars of the community such as priests and ministers and Little League coaches have become notorious for being involved in sexual encounters with their charges. The point here—and we can't stress this enough—is that when it comes to the possibility of sexual abuse of our children, trust no one!

Sexual Abuse: Effects and Remedies

Even though the threat of abuse is pervasive, many of us parents do not comprehend the significance of protecting our children because we're still ignorant about the long-lasting emotional damage such abuse can bring about. The physical damage is often brutal enough, but the psychological damage could be worse and may not surface until much later. The more common effects of sexual abuse include depression, anxiety, and self-destructive behaviors such as suicidal gestures—and many of these symptoms might linger well into adulthood. There have been many cases in which abused children become precocious and even sexually aggressive toward other children. The long-term effects of sexual abuse also include poor self-esteem, bad marriages, drug and alcohol abuse, and a confusion of self that often casts the childhood victim as an adult sexual predator.

Sexuality is a normal part of human life and an essential component of the maturation process. When a child is exposed to sexual stimuli prematurely and forcefully, their normal sexual and emotional maturation becomes interrupted and distorted, with destructive effects on other aspects of their social and psychological functioning. As a result, they develop a damaged psyche, which leads to a myriad of psychological problems and poor coping mechanisms. For example, psychological studies have proven that even the root of many eating disorders may be a child's attempt to regain control of his or her body after being violated.

Victims of sexual abuse are not alone in using faulty coping mechanisms. Parents and other family members are often guilty, too. Finding out that a child has been traumatized in this way may be so painful for a parent, let's say, that it results in the denial of the significance of the abuse, or even that it occurred. When this happens, the child's needs are often ignored, or not taken seriously. In some cases, in subtle ways, the child is blamed for the abuse, which naturally creates even more psychological problems for this boy or girl.

So, what can practical parents do to safeguard their children? Well, you would hope that your child would come right out and tell you when something untoward is going on, but the research suggests this will not happen. That's why it's important to watch for signs that may signal some sexual abuse. This is especially true with very young children who do not yet know how to verbalize that they're being violated. In fact, many victims are too young to realize that what's happening is wrong. It's your responsibility as a parent to learn to recognize the behavioral symptoms of a child who is being sexually abused. If your child suddenly becomes obsessed with talking about sex, for example, or becomes sexually provocative with other children, it's probably a warning that something troubling is going on. Some children may begin to masturbate frequently. In some cases, little girls will become overly friendly in a physical way with male adults. Such instances of sexual acting out do not always signal a sexual trauma, but they are usually a prompt for parents to start paying attention of one kind or another.

When children are unable to verbalize that they've been sexually abused, or that they're currently involved in an abusive situation, their emotional trauma can result in both behavioral and academic dysfunction. A child who has been, for the most part, well behaved, may change overnight into exhibiting such problems. The child may become unruly and defy adult authority. As part of this defiant behavior, the child may become either very nervous, manic, or extremely depressed, sometimes with talk of suicide. The behavior problem will invariably carry over into school, where you might begin to receive negative reports on your child's interactions with students and teachers. It's possible you will also begin to see a sharp drop in grades, accompanied by a lack of interest in school and related social activities.

Sexually abused children may begin avoiding certain situations, locations, or persons. They may also refuse to participate in certain activities. This may be an attempt to escape from or avoid the person who molested them, or the situation and location in which it happened. This type of avoidance can be a very strong warning sign that something has happened, especially if the children get upset when questioned.

If you had an open, close relationship with your children that quickly transforms into something secretive and off-putting, they're probably sending out signals that something is happening and that they have some fear of being discovered. Realize that a manipulating sexual predator may be forcing these kids to keep secrets in order to control their behavior and keep the illicit activity from being exposed. Coercion may also be part of the abuse, in which the predator is threatening to kill the child, or maybe a parent or other family member.

Perhaps most alarming are those situations where children are being sexually abused and there's no overt discomfort manifested in their behavior. This can happen when the children have been convinced by the predators that what they're doing is perfectly normal. Keep your eye on any close relationships forming between your children and any adult, including neighbors, family friends, teachers, bosses, or mentors. It's a practical precaution to keep your kids from spending an inordinate amount of time alone with any adult, especially in unsupervised settings.

Recently, there have been a number of prominent cases in which teachers have been accused of molesting students in classrooms. In almost every case, one teacher was paired with one student, with no other students or teachers present, after school hours. In today's hypervigilant climate, few professionals will place themselves in a situation where they are alone with a student in a secluded place, or without other people within earshot, to avoid perceptions of impropriety.

When it comes down to it, no one knows your child better than you do, so if your practical instincts tip you off to any indicators of sexual abuse, or if you know for sure that something has happened, you must take the following actions immediately:

- Sit down with your children and discuss the incident(s). Stay calm. The last thing you want is to intimidate your children or make them think they're in trouble. No matter how anxious you are to know the truth, give your children some breathing room.

- Contact the police and relay all the information you have. Try to keep from becoming hysterical, as you will only impede the report-taking process. If the sexually abused child is a girl, request that the police officer assigned to question her be a female from a sex crimes unit. She will be specially trained, and sensitive to the needs of a female victim.

- Take your child to the hospital for a complete physical examination. If you have a daughter, make sure that the examining physician is experienced at performing gynecological rape evaluations. The doctor will be much gentler during what will be an emotionally and physically traumatic examination for your child.

- Your child should receive immediate rape crisis counseling. Your family should also consider group psychotherapy sessions to discuss the traumatic event, because it *does* affect the whole family. If the pedophile is a member of the family, he should not be included in the family sessions immediately; he should be working on his own therapy first. Eventually, he can be integrated into the family sessions, especially if the family unit will stay together after this tragedy.

- If the predator turns out to be a boyfriend, husband, uncle, or any other family member, get him out of the house immediately! If the predator is a minor, have him move in with another relative or friend (who has no minor children in the household), or place him in a private or government supported therapeutic group home. Do not allow a second incident to occur. The predator will need treatment. Make it clear to anyone in a position of authority that with or without a jail sentence, he definitely needs help!

- If you suspect sexual abuse against a child who is not in your home, you should immediately contact your local child-protection agency. You may feel guilty doing this, especially if you aren't sure, but a child's life and emotional stability may hang in the balance.

Prevention is always the best method of protection. Just as we inoculate our children against disease, we can help them be strong enough to avoid or even fend off sexual predators. The following are nine practical parenting strategies you can use to protect your children. They will also help you teach them how to deal with any situation in which they may be seduced, attacked, or placed in mortal danger by a sexual predator.

Nine Ways to Protect Your Children

1. As early as your children can understand speech, teach them about appropriate and inappropriate physical activity. Let them know that their private parts are *private,* and should not be touched by anyone except a doctor or a designated parent who may be washing them or giving them a bath. You don't want to scare them, but at the same time, they must be aware of the dangers of the world, especially in this regard.

2. Be aware of your own behavior and how it might influence your children's view of sexuality. Bathing with a child up to the age of two or three might be okay. However, continuing to do so with an older child can be inappropriate. You don't want your children thinking that it's normal for adults and children to be naked together, especially in intimate situations.

3. Keep your children under your wing for as long as you can, especially before the age of seven. Quite normally, your children will sometimes ask for permission to eat dinner at a friend's home, or sleep there overnight. If you allow such privileges, make sure that you have been in that home yourself, to scout out any potentially troubling situations, such as teenage siblings of the opposite sex or family members who might drink heavily. Go with your gut, but make sure there's always a responsible adult present to act as baby-sitter and chaperone.

4. Allow no adult to live or spend time in your home who is a serious drug and/or alcohol user. Again, alcohol and drugs are at the root of the majority of sexual abuse cases; this is especially true in cases of incest. It's always the same excuse given by the father, uncle, or boyfriend who's arrested for molesting a child: "I was drunk." "I was high." "I just didn't know what I was doing." The phrases are all too familiar, and you don't want to hear them in connection to your own children.

5. If your children are developing a close relationship with an adult, such as a teacher, community leader, family member, or family friend, keep an eagle eye on what's taking place between them. Get to know all the adults with whom your children are emotionally close. Be conservative and cautious. When guests stay at home, unless they're the closest of family friends, it's often a good idea to have your own kids sleep in your bedroom, or to bunk together, on the theory that there's safety in numbers.

6. Be aware of what your children are doing on the Internet. We've been hearing an awful lot lately about children being lured to sexual predators through e-mail and private chat rooms. For very young children, especially, it's often a good idea to keep them from private chat rooms, unless they're being monitored by you at the time. Let them surf the commercial sites instead. There are many useful public-service brochures available on how to supervise your children's use of the Internet, including how to avoid predators on the Web, which you can obtain by writing to: Child Safety on the Information Highway; National Center for Missing and Exploited Children, 8403 Colesville Road, Suite 865, Silver Spring, MD 20910.

7. If you're enrolling your children in day care, make sure that it's licensed and that all personnel have been fingerprinted and criminal checks have been conducted. Request a list of parents who have had their children in the center, and call for references. If you use a private baby-sitter, find someone who has impeccable credentials and comes highly recommended. Ask friends to refer someone they've used and liked; it's better not to take a chance on a complete stranger.

8. Always accompany your children to public rest-room facilities. By doing so, you can ensure that no offender follows your kids or is waiting inside to invade their privacy and abuse them. Also, ensure that the facility is sanitary for your child to use.

9. Do role-plays using different situations in which your children might be lured or seduced by a pedophile. Pretend to be a neighbor who invites your children to enter his house to play with a puppy. First, ask your children to explain the dangers of this situation. Second, ask them to come up with ways to say no. For example, they could politely tell the neighbor that they're not allowed to go to anyone's home without their mom or dad. If the neighbor tries to snatch them into the house, they should scream "Help!" at the top of their lungs.

   Employ many different situations, such as a teacher asking a student to sit close to them in an empty classroom, or even a motorist asking for directions. Throughout the role-plays, continue to encourage your children to generate different behaviors or strategies to stay safe. Remember, you want to teach your children how to think on their feet. Chances are, you're not going to be there to protect your kids when they encounter a sexual predator, and they must know how to keep themselves out of harmful situations.

Jeff: Montel had an opportunity a number of years back to interview a serial child molester named Wesley Allen Dodd, who was convicted of murder and eventually hung for his crimes in Walla Walla State Prison, in Washington. In the last weeks of his life, Dodd reached out to Montel from Death Row, wanting to come clean on some of his stalking methods, ostensibly to alert parents to the behavior of other molesters in their communities. He was also trying to impress the judge and win a stay of execution with this public display of contrition, but Montel and his producers didn't care about that. They just wanted to present this sick man's insights as a public service to their viewers—and they did.

So Montel sat in a room with this miscreant for almost four hours. They were separated by glass, but it still felt to Montel as if he were sitting next to the devil incarnate. (There wasn't enough hot water in the entire state of Washington to wash away the slime Montel felt in his pores after the interview!) And yet it was worth all that stomach-turning trouble to hear what this man had to share. He boasted that at 19 years old, he could have walked onto any playground in America and determined which child in that playground had the lowest self-esteem. The child playing off by himself, often with his head down, barely interacting with the other kids—that was the child this man targeted. He said he could get a kid like that off the playground in less than three minutes. He knew how to be nice, how to push the right buttons, and how to counter every poorly programmed argument the parents had placed into this child.

Think about that for a moment. If an uneducated, unstable lunatic can so quickly spot the easy marks, either he's doing something horribly right or the parents are doing something horribly wrong—or both. Think about how your own children present themselves. Do they carry themselves with confidence and intelligence? Or do they shrink from the scene, head in hands, with the weak posture of an easy victim? Help them to feel good enough about themselves so that their demeanor can truly reflect their personality.

Man, this creep had it all figured out. He even scripted little scenes in his head to get a feel for how they'd go . . .

"Mommy said not to talk to strangers."

"Oh, but I'm not a stranger. If I were a stranger, would I tell you my name? My name is Mike. What's your name?"

"Billy."

"Great, Billy. Now we're not strangers. Strangers are people you don't know. Now we're friends."

He had an entire routine he used to pull, where he tried to get a child to help him look for a lost puppy, and he played these kids out. That's what he did, he played them. He knew how they'd been programmed by their schools and their parents, and he counter-programmed them to where they were virtually help-less against him. The man was scum, but he knew what he was doing, and we as parents must always know what scum like Wesley Allen Dodd are doing. They're out there all the time, try-ing to out-think us, to out-think our children. And the best defense against them is to raise healthy, stable, alert children who know enough to follow not only the letter of your teaching, but the spir-it as well.

◆ ◆ ◆ ◆ ◆

Life is complicated and busy. We know that. We know you might not have the time to use all the practical parenting measures we've described in this chapter. But there *is* a technique that you can use that only takes a few minutes a day: communication. Talk to your children—plainly, openly, and often. Let them know that they can tell you anything—anything at all—especially when it comes to situations that are embarrassing, unusual, or unpleasant.

Absolutely, the best way to get your children to be honest with you is by keeping the lines of communication open at all times. Let your kids know that you are *always* available to listen, especially in situations like these, and that you listen with *no* value judgments. When you build trust, your children will come to you!

The Enemy We Know

Susie was a bright, precocious ten-year-old. Pretty. Energetic. Caring. As far as her mother, Theresa, could tell, she was doing all right—especially considering the hand she'd been dealt. The little girl's biological father had spent time in jail for nonpayment of child support, but things were basically okay.

At a family picnic one summer afternoon, Susie approached her mother, complaining that her belly itched. Theresa thought that was a bit strange. The child was very specific. It wasn't a stomachache. Her belly itched. Theresa lifted the little girl's blouse and discovered what she could only describe as stretch marks. If she didn't know any better, she'd have thought her daughter was pregnant.

But that was precisely the problem. Theresa didn't know any better, and Susie was five months pregnant. Five months pregnant! A ten-year-old girl! The father was the 18-year-old nephew of Theresa's fiancé, a young man Theresa had taken into her home after his apartment had been destroyed in a fire. She had done so without a thought. The boy's uncle was about to become her husband. The boy's mother was one of her closest friends. The boy was like family. How could you not take someone in under circumstances like those? Theresa even allowed the boy to baby-sit her little girl. A turn of events like this was about the last thing she ever expected.

Predictably, it was the last thing Susie expected, too.

At ten, she didn't truly know what it meant to be sexually active. Forget truly; she didn't know the first thing. She didn't know what sexual intercourse was, or that it was a thing to be avoided until she was older. She didn't know how babies were made. She didn't understand the changes going on in her body. In fact, the first conversation Theresa had with her daughter about sex was her attempt to explain to Susie what had happened to her. Some of these things came out in courtroom testimony, and some of these things came out in a wrenching interview on Montel's show—and yet they all painted a disturbing picture of a woman so cluelessly out of touch with her child that their lives together would never again be the same.

Theresa might have done a better job of parenting, and she might have seen some of the changes in her daughter's behavior. For one thing, Susie had gotten her period at nine—well on the early side—so there was plenty of opportunity to explain what was happening to her body in terms she might understand. For another, the little girl had been depressed for several weeks. Theresa had held several conferences with her teachers to try to determine the root cause of the problem. She even took Susie to the family doctor to see if there was some hormonal reason for the depression. Theresa had noticed that the child's periods had become irregular, and she worried that there might be some connection between the irregularity and the depression. Her eyes were open to the problem, but she still couldn't see.

When the doctor turned up nothing, Theresa took Susie home and resumed their routine, and it wasn't until several weeks later at the family picnic that Theresa learned the alarming truth. She called the police so that they might act against her fiancé's nephew, but it didn't take long for Theresa's fitness as a mother to be called into question. How was it possible, the court wondered, for a mother not to notice that her ten-year-old daughter was five months pregnant? How can a "mature" child not be made to understand what it means to get her period? How can a teenage boy be allowed to spend such large amounts of unsupervised time with a pretty little girl?

Certainly, the boy needed some help, and Susie would need some counseling as well as immediate medical attention, but the case was made that the true villain of this unusual family drama was Theresa. It was her failure as a parent that left the door open.

Naturally, the family was torn apart by this devastating situation. Susie delivered a healthy baby, which is now in state care. Susie, too, was taken from her mother's home. Theresa and her close friend, the boy's mother, became locked in a bitter legal battle. Her marriage was put on hold. And Susie's deadbeat father returned to fight for custody of the child he had once ignored.

The lesson? The story seems too terrible to believe— and the knee-jerk response, from the outside looking in, is that nothing remotely resembling this can ever happen to us. But that's nonsense. Bad things happen to good people all the time. The key is to cover all of your bases, and push the percentages as far in your favor as possible. It's never too soon to talk to your kids about sex—and if their bodies are telling you they're ready to have the conversation, it's sometimes too late. And it's not always enough to trust our adult friendships to yield trusting relationships for our children. Theresa didn't truly know this young man she naively allowed into her home. She knew his background, she knew his family, but she didn't know *him*. And that's an unacceptable mistake to make where your own children are concerned.

It's one thing to take precautions, and quite another to throw caution to the wind, which seems to have been what happened in this tragic case. Theresa—and Susie, too, in a far more fundamental way—learned that it's never enough to trust your friends' instincts, just as it's never a good idea to put off a conversation your child is ready to have simply because you're not ready to start it.

◆ ◆ ◆

···CHAPTER···
NINE

SEX AND THE PRACTICAL PARENT

If you're like us, you probably caught that Salt 'n' Pepa video, "Let's Talk About Sex," and found yourself thinking that your kids would soon be in a world of trouble—if they weren't in that world already. The video, like so much of today's music, movies, and magazines aimed at teens, revealed that a lot of young people were sexually active, and that *active* was perhaps too tame a word to describe what was going on.

Indeed, the numbers are high. According to the Commission on Adolescent Sexual Health, 75 percent of boys and 50 percent of girls aged 15 to 19 have engaged in sexual intercourse. As practical parents, we find those numbers depressingly high—and, even more depressing, the statistics are substantially greater for sex play or heavy petting. Naturally, these big numbers have brought big problems, proving that our kids have not only been irresponsible, but reckless with their health and their futures. Many are getting into trouble through unexpected and unwanted pregnancies, while others are coming down with sexually transmitted diseases in record numbers.

Despite HIV educational initiatives targeted at children of all ages, a Tale University Center for Interdisciplinary Research on AIDS study reports that nearly nine out of ten American young people still remain in denial and do not think that they can easily get HIV through heterosexual sex. But they do. They also get syphilis and gonorrhea. And, they also get pregnant.

Kids Having Sex

Children making choices about sex without proper parental guidance is like these same kids playing Russian roulette—with a six-shooter loaded with *five* bullets! The odds of a positive outcome are not good. And yet parental involvement continues to lag. A 1998 *Time*/CNN telephone poll found that 45 percent of American teenagers are learning about sex from friends, 29 percent are getting their principal information from television, and fewer than 8 percent are being educated by parents and schools.

Clearly, we can draw a straight line from the high rates of sexually transmitted diseases and teen pregnancies to the widespread failings of our sexual education at school and in the home. Sex is far more complicated than "gettin' it on" or "knockin' boots," and runaway sexual ignorance results in some very unhealthy practices and behaviors. We've counseled many young people in this area, and have come away with the following disturbing conclusions:

— *Unprotected sex is still rampant.* Again, many kids simply don't think they can contract the HIV virus from heterosexual sex. They think it can only happen to drug users and homosexuals.

— *Kids use condoms improperly.* The availability and social acceptance of condoms has in many ways promoted safer sex, as if the mere presence of a condom is a free pass to move forward. But when kids *do* use condoms, they often use them improperly. For example, they might reach for a jar of petroleum jelly to use as a lubricant, without realizing that petroleum jelly actually eats through the rubber. With proper education, they would learn that if a lubricant is needed, they should reach instead for a water-based jelly, such as the K-Y brand.

— *Kids use the wrong condoms.* Not all condoms are created equal. Some offer better protection from venereal disease than others. There are still kids (as well as adults, we should point out) who favor lambskin condoms, and while it's true that these offer greater sensitivity, they are also more porous. Unmarried couples should only use condoms made from latex.

— *Risky sex is everywhere.* In some communities, anal sex, known as "deep impact," has become a popular, presumably safe alternative to sexual intercourse. The kids are correct in thinking that you can't get pregnant this way, but the risk of HIV or AIDS increases tremendously with anal sex. This is due to the simple fact that the anus has less elasticity than the vagina and is much more likely to tear and bleed. Every available piece of research confirms that the blood-to-sperm connection is the best conduit for the transmission of HIV.

— *Multiple-partnering has become a kind of sport.* We've interviewed hundreds of teenagers who've attended "hooky parties," where they skip school and have group sex in a home that is unattended by a parent. As if this weren't enough, these gatherings are usually punctuated by pot and alcohol, and the use of these chemicals results in impaired judgment and less caution in safer sex practices.

— *There are many young girls who misinform their partners in order to become pregnant.* This is a sad fact of life in many neighborhoods, where young girls might feel unloved by their parents and cast aside by their peers. They mistakenly believe that if they become pregnant, they'll finally have someone they can love, who will love them back. They don't stop to consider that they're totally unprepared for such a turn—emotionally, educationally, or financially. More and more, parents are discovering these "hidden pregnancies" late in their daughters' terms. Typically, these babies having babies do not seek prenatal care, even if it's available, placing both mother and child at risk of illness and complications.

Understand, it's not just ignorance that's at the root of the problem of youth sex. Many of our kids feel invulnerable, as if the problems discussed in school or in the media don't apply to them. Their increasing promiscuity has as much to do with curiosity as it does with rebellion, but it also flows from an unspoken permissiveness that has taken hold in our culture. Think about it: TV and magazine ads promote sex and fun as pieces of the same pie. Billboards present young people in various stages of undress. Remember the Calvin Klein campaign that featured prepubescent boys and girls in their underwear? What was up with *that*? Even in movies and television, sexual images and sexuality abound, convincing young children that it's okay to have a boyfriend or girlfriend before they even finish kindergarten!

And you can just forget about the music industry. You've probably seen some of the rap or hip-hop videos your kids typically check out. Admit it, those videos are so sexually explicit that they even turn *you* on! The rapper Sisqó has so many chicks waving their backsides at him in that "th-th-th-thong-thong" song, we sometimes can't decide whether to keep watching or take Dramamine. The lyrics are no better than the accompanying images: "I want to sex you up." "Give me that thang." "I want to do it to ya 'til ya scream!" If all of this doesn't seem like a recipe for the sexual charging-up of our children, then chickens *do* have lips.

Another explanation for our children's early sexuality is simple biology. Many scientists theorize that our kids are maturing much faster than we did. Girls are getting their periods at age nine and ten. Boys are reaching puberty soon after. They're also growing taller and faster than ever before. It's now hard to tell the difference between some 12-year-olds and some 20-year-olds. Some believe that this change in growth pattern is related to the hormones in the foods we eat, and if there's one thing our kids love to do, it's eat!

Whatever the reasons, the fact remains that our kids are sexually active—and at a much earlier age than ever before. And the kids who are not already active are pressured to start. Perhaps the strongest pressure comes from friends or peers. As with any other behavior, not just sexual, kids cave in to peer pressure because they believe that if they don't "do it," they won't be accepted by their friends, or may be even rejected by a boyfriend or girlfriend—and sometimes these concerns are justified.

Discussing Sex with Your Teenage Kids

Sex is a natural part of life. As children grow, sexuality becomes a maturational, developmental, and psychological border that must be met and crossed. If we want them to journey safely, we must teach them to be responsible. We must teach them about sex. The late Dr. Mary S. Calderone, a physician, a pioneering advocate of sexual education, and the co-founder of the Sex Information and Educational Council of the United States, spent her life convincing parents that children need to be taught about sex. She was right, but a lot of us still have trouble with the teaching part. We're uncomfortable with the subject, possibly because many of our own parents treated sex as a taboo subject that required no discussion.

We must break this generational dysfunction and be forthcoming with our teens about sexuality in order for them to see sex as an essential part of life that must be treated with careful thought and the highest regard. Teaching and discussing sex with our children is the best way to help them recognize their own sexuality in a normal, healthy, and responsible manner.

We're the first to admit it: Talking to your kids about sex can be tough. One of the contributing difficulties might be some pre-existing communications problems, which make talking about something as personal as sex seem impossible. Also, we parents may be inhibited and have somewhat antiquated views on sexuality, but this is the time to bite the bullet and do the deed. Commit to the conversation, and the words will follow—and to help you along, we offer some of our own experience:

— *Structure your talks around your teens' concerns.* When it comes to having "the talk," it's sometimes hard to know where to begin. However, there is a practical parenting strategy you can use when speaking with your teen on this topic, which we call the listen-and-respond technique. Strike up any normal or neutral conversation with your teen, and actively *listen* for any questions, concerns, or references about sex or sexuality. Next, *respond* to the question or the concern with your own question or statement, which will draw out your teen's concern. This is an excellent way to directly address those areas of sexuality that your teen needs to talk about. Here's an example of a listen-and-respond scenario that Jeff presented to a patient, which this mother utilized in a family session:

Teen: I saw an article in the paper today about an abortion doctor who was killed by a sniper. People said he was killing unborn babies.

Mom: What do you think about abortion? Is it right or wrong?

Teen: I think if a girl were to get pregnant, she should have the right to choose what to do.

Mom: If that girl got pregnant and was under age, do you think she should consult with her mom and dad?

Teen: I definitely think she should speak to her mom.

Mom: What do you think her mom can do to make it more comfortable for her to speak about pregnancy?

Teen: I think her mom should let her know that it's okay to talk about anything, especially getting pregnant.

Mom: What sorts of things do you think I could tell you that might keep you from getting into that same situation?

The mother was able to engage in a conversation about sex with her daughter by responding to her questions and concerns about a neutral event with her own questions and comments, whereupon she was finally able to gear the conversation toward a more personal situation. Practice the listen-and-respond technique with your teen every single day, and you'll soon discover that you don't have to go looking for openings in your kids' questions; those openings will come to *you*.

— *Always keep in mind that sexuality is part of life.* Parents often treat developing adolescent and teen sexuality as a stage that is inconvenient and foreboding. This negative attitude can easily influence the type of communication, or *noncommunication*, established between a parent and a teenager. It can also cause our children to develop an unhealthy attitude about sexuality, which can be as dangerous as being uninformed. Therefore, it's extremely important for parents to always keep in mind that our children's developing sexuality is a healthy and natural part of their lives.

Parents should also remember that sexuality is much more than just "doin' it." For many of us, it's the basic foundation of health and happiness. To repress its expression or view it as unnatural will inevitably lead to long-term emotional conflicts, which will in turn affect future interpersonal relationships, such as friendships and marriage. Educating and speaking to our children about sex should become a family tradition and responsibility— one that should be approached with enthusiasm and not dread.

— *Get educated about sex.* It starts with you, and it ends with you, and if you don't know what you're talking about, your kids will suffer. A lot of things our kids are dealing with today, especially HIV, were not part of our generational concerns. Learn about all sexually transmitted diseases, including herpes, viral warts, and Hepatitis C. Also, research the best protection that's available. Consult your family doctor. Read parenting and youth-oriented magazines for the latest information on what "generation next" is thinking. One such magazine, *React,* which is distributed to schools throughout the country, emphasizes a healthy lifestyle, sexual responsibility, and active communication with parents. There are plenty of television movies and after-school specials that address these issues, so seek them out. On-line, you can log on to popular sites such as Yahoo, which posts daily information on teenagers and their dating habits.

— *Insist that sex education become part of your child's school curriculum.* Become a partner in the sex education process, and an extension of that process at home. Review the curriculum, and if at all possible, sit in on one of the sex education classes to determine the quality of the information and the attitude of the teacher as well. Back in the day when we attended high school, sexual education classes were a joke, often taught by a gym teacher instead of a trained health professional. The classes were long on issues of hygiene—particularly concerning the sex organs—short on birth control, and pretty much devoid of everything in between. Proper sexual education should be comprehensive, addressing both the physical and emotional aspects of sexuality. Discuss with the teachers those aspects of sexual education that you deem most important. You might also find that the more formal approach taken by the schools can be helpful in providing a comprehensive education, whereas the parental approach might be a little more hit-and-miss. Somewhere in the balance you'll find a way to connect with your teen.

— *Recognize the power of peer pressure.* As you establish an open dialogue with your children, especially when discussing sex, always recognize that they're facing tremendous pressure from their friends and others to go along for the ride. In your talks, explore any ideas your teens may have about sex and how many of those ideas come from their friends. Discuss whether there are pressures regarding sexual activity in order to fit in. And, of course, offer solutions and options that will help your children become individuals and make independent and responsible decisions about sex.

— *Present a united front.* Quite often, parents allow one adult partner in the relationship to do all the talking and educating about sex. Even if the one parent who does the talking is really good at it, this is not the best approach. If possible, both parents should become a team when it comes to discussing this subject. We're not suggesting that you gang up on your children and out-number them two-to-one in each conversation, but take turns. Each parent should have something to offer in this area. In the first place, it gives the child more balanced information, from both an adult male and an adult female perspective. And, since much of sex is about relationships, the team effort is a living demonstration of a man and woman working together around issues of sexuality. Finally, both parents can support one another as well as generate different approaches and ideas to working with the child. Sexual education really should be a family activity.

— *Avoid double standards.* Remember the 1970s movie *The Mack?* The Mack had money, the Mack had the *jewels* (both kinds!), and the Mack had all the women! To many black men who came of age during that period, the Mack was "the man." Well, let's change with the times, gentlemen. The Mack is dead, and yet his legacy lives on. Come on, guys, admit it! When your sons talk about their girlfriends, or when they bring a new person home for you to meet, you're secretly feeling pretty good about things. You're proudly thinking, *That's my son*, or *The apple doesn't fall from the tree!* But you know what? Your kids pick up on that attitude, however subtle it may be. What message does this convey to our sons? Not a good one, that's for sure. They begin to internalize this praise as positive reinforcement for polygamous relationships, and they start to equate sex with conquest.

Now, on the flip side, when your daughters talk about boys or they bring home a new boyfriend, male parents go postal! The message our daughters elicit from this response is that it's wrong or sinful to have relationships with boys. So check your sexist attitudes and behaviors at the door, and teach your sons to be respectful of women by discussing the equality of the sexes, and perhaps advocating serial monogamy in dating. And cut your daughters some slack!

There has been no more telling response to this upswing in teenage promiscuity than the concurrent rise in the number of parents advocating abstinence for their children. To our thinking, though, this is just an easy way around a tough problem, not unlike staying home when it rains instead of investing in a raincoat or umbrella. If you think that your child is sexually active, then whatever your beliefs or values, sexual education must include learning about safe sex practices first, and abstinence second. You've got to put out the fire before you start rebuilding the house. On the other hand, if your child has *not* been sexually active, then you can certainly emphasize the value of abstinence. To cover all bases, teach both abstinence *and* safe sex.

Yes, abstaining is the safest way for your children to stay out of situations they can't handle. But if they have to go there, send them in with as much knowledge as possible. It has been our experience that children who learn about sexuality in an open and unbiased manner usually choose abstinence. Why? Because sex is not just about love and hormones; it's also about knowing how to set priorities and acting responsibly. If you teach your children to respect others and themselves, they will make the right decision when the time comes.

At some point, you reach a time and place in your life as a parent where you can't *make* the decisions for your kids, but you *can* prepare for that time and place by teaching your children to choose wisely.

The Girl Who Cried Wolf

Alyssa, a 16-year-old girl, was raised in a moral town, by a moral family. She went to church with her family every single Sunday. They gave a blessing over every fami-ly meal. She was a dutiful student, a responsible daughter, and a trusted friend and neighbor. By every outward stan-dard (and by most of the inward ones, too) she was a good girl.

There was only one aspect of Alyssa's life that gave her parents cause for concern. She had a boyfriend. There was nothing wrong with the boy himself—in fact, he was from a good family and was a polite young man—but Alyssa's parents didn't think she was old enough for steady dating. There would be time for that later, they said, after high school. They had no idea that their daughter was sexually active; such a thing was unthinkable.

Alyssa became pregnant, and she was so ashamed and confused by this turn of events that she spun the kind of story that we usually find in fairy tales. She told her parents she'd been raped. She couldn't face telling them the truth— that she had brought this on herself—and thought it would be easier to hide behind a brutal assault than a public betrayal of the values they had worked so hard to instill. She didn't want to cause any more embarrassment to the family than she already had, and in desperation, this is what she came up with.

It might have been a viable strategy but for the way the story spun out of control. As a religious person, Alyssa told her parents she wanted to keep the baby. Her parents were anti-abortion, but the thought of keeping a child conceived in rape was an abomination. Surely, they pleaded, she could at least put the child up for adoption, but Alyssa wanted to raise the child. She wouldn't hear of giving up the baby.

Meanwhile, as the story spread, the town leaders grew concerned. Was there a rapist running loose in their community? Were other young girls in danger? It never occurred to anyone that Alyssa was lying, so the assumption was that everyone else was at risk until the perpetrator was apprehended. Alyssa offered a description to the police in order to maintain the charade; she was even interviewed by local media, as the search continued for a "suspect." Everywhere she turned, it seemed, people offered a supportive shoulder, and Alyssa felt enormously guilty about it, but she stuck to her story just the same.

At some point, Alyssa's fabricated story came to the attention of producers at the Montel *show. It wasn't every day that a young rape victim insisted on carrying a resulting pregnancy to term. She was asked to appear on the show with her family, to talk to other pregnant rape victims who were considering keeping their children. It was a powerful segment, but the power seemed to flow mostly from the other girls, not from Alyssa. Montel's radar kicked in, and he started asking Alyssa some very specific questions. She squirmed a little at first, got herself snagged in a lie or two, and then she broke down and told her story.*

It was a gripping moment—to see this beautiful, scared child break down in such a public way—but her spirits seemed to lift as she came clean. It was a story she had dreaded sharing with her closest friends and family, and here she was talking about it on national television. As she spoke, it was as if a great weight was being lifted from her shoulders.

Her parents were aghast, but at the same time they appeared somewhat relieved. Alyssa's admission answered a great many questions surrounding their daughter's pregnancy and her decision to keep the child.

After the show, the family returned to their small, moral town to pick up the pieces and seek therapy. Friends and neighbors were quick to forgive Alyssa her charade—possibly because, deep down, they wondered how their own children would have reacted to a similar set of circumstances. Alyssa never intended for her lie to grow as big as it did. She never meant to hurt anyone. Mostly, she did it to protect her parents from the truth—and to protect herself from their disappointment.

◆ ◆ ◆

···CHAPTER···
TEN

DIVORCE AND THE PRACTICAL PARENT

Here's a stunner: 64 percent of all marriages that began in 1990 ended in divorce by the turn of the millennium. And that's just in the first ten years. Who knows how many couples will be standing after the next ten?

What's especially unsettling about these numbers is that they set down in hard terms some of the pervasive, anecdotal observations many of us have collected on divorce, and the general splintering of the American family. Look behind the runaway divorce rate and you'll see what strikes us as an even more disturbing statistic: 70 percent of those failed marriages produced at least one child. Wow! That means that more children than ever before are being born into soon-to-be-broken homes. Throw in the disappointing ten-year period surrounding 1990, and the numbers look much the same, to where roughly half of all children born in this country over the past 15 years have ended up being children of divorce.

What was once an aberration has now become routine.

Clearly, we could never hope to address the complicated and varied issues of parenting and divorce in a single chapter, and we don't set out to offer any kind of comprehensive text on what to expect from these rough patches. There's far too much ground to cover in a single volume, let alone a single chapter. But we do mean to share some thoughts and observations on the theme, just as we have done throughout this book. We'll leave the far-reaching societal implications to others, along with the long-term, day-to-day guideposts for divorced parents, and focus instead on what we believe to be some of the central pieces of the fallout.

How do you talk to your kids about what's about to happen? Once you and your spouse have come to the regrettable but unavoidable decision to call it quits, how do you sell the notion to your children? *When* are they old enough to understand? *What*, precisely, are they old enough to understand? What do you need to do to keep your kids emotionally healthy through such an emotionally destructive process?

The current state of divorce is almost always ugly. Matrimonial litigation in this country is predetermined to be ugly. That's what it's become—an adversarial, take-no-prisoners system—and there's often no getting around it. Even husbands and wives vowing to remain amicable are at each other's throats before it's all over. Step into the camp of your attorneys, and things will almost always turn volatile and nasty, and it's that nastiness that you and your ex are going to have to work double-time to keep from spilling over onto your children.

Stop and think about the swirl building up around you. If your relationship has deteriorated to where you need a third-party mediator or a contentious litigation to divvy up the spoils or mete out custody arrangements, then surely some of that tension has been passed along to your children. Certainly, there's been some damage with respect to the way they regard their mother and father, and their relationship to each—the kind of damage that cannot be so easily repaired.

The Effects of Divorce on the Kids

Let's backtrack a bit and overstate the obvious. In a divorce, it's absolutely imperative that both parents focus their full attentions on the mess they're making for their children. We're not suggesting that you stay together for the sake of the kids, but what we *are* imploring you to do is to get your baggage out of the way before you interact with your children. Set it aside. Don't let what's been poisoned between two adults also poison the essential relationship that remains with parent and child. Too often, parents spend more time fighting with each other than paying attention to the needs of their children—and this at a time that could possibly be the most destructive in a child's life.

Kids who've been battle-scarred by divorce don't do as well in school as they might have; they don't have the emotional troubleshooting skills of their peers; they've given back chunks of their confidence and self-esteem. They're handicapped, in a very real way, by some of the very poor choices made by their parents. On the other hand, kids who've sailed through a divorce without incident tend to perform as well as their counterparts from traditional, two-parent, still-married households.

Take the contention out of the house. Completely. If things have gotten to the point where you and your spouse can no longer stand civilly in the same room with each other, *find a way* to stand civilly in the same room with each other. As we said, set your baggage aside and deal with your child. Respect certain boundaries. Agree not to scream at one another, or to blame one another in front of the kids. Pledge a sacred oath never to use your children as weapons, or to play one relationship against another. Find a way to communicate what's going on to your children in ways they might understand. It doesn't matter if your child is only a year old, he or she needs to be told, by both of you, in a loving way, as a family.

Typically, at the end of many marriages, it falls to the mother to explain the situation to the children, but we're here to tell those abdicating fathers to just sit their butts back down and deal with their kids. Treat them with respect. Do your job. Be there for your children. No matter what. We don't care how angry you are at your partner—don't take it out on your kids!

Jeff: When Montel and his second wife decided to split, they sat down with their two young children and spelled things out for them. It was a profoundly sad, yet truly loving moment. Each parent took turns holding each child. At one point, Montel II and Wynter-Grace were both in Montel's lap; at another, they were both with their mother. It wasn't an orchestrated thing, but the back-and-forth between mother and father was a physical, tangible way for the kids to feel loved, to know that as much as things were going to be different, they would also be a little bit the same. They'd all be able to reach out for each other and hold each other, as before. Mom and Dad weren't going to disappear.

The conversation followed the usual path: No, the fact that we can't live together in no way changes the way we feel about you; no, it's not your fault; yes, we will always be a family. Wynter-Grace didn't really understand the term *divorce*, but she got the concept. How could she *not* get the concept? Even at five years old, so many of her little friends had already been through the same motions that she knew the deal. But more than what was said was *how* it was said, and it was said with love and care and compassion. In fact, Mom and Dad were so careful to keep the tension between them from spreading throughout the house that the kids were really surprised by this turn of events. The adults had been going back and forth for months; they'd done their fair share of hollering and crying—but they managed to do it behind closed doors, away from the children. The children had no idea.

We don't mean to diminish the importance of *what* was said— in Montel's house, or in yours—we just want to highlight the importance of *how* it was said. The *what* is also significant, and perhaps the most significant aspect of the conversation is the universal question of blame. It comes up in virtually every divorce. It's incredibly important for kids to hear they're not at fault. In almost every case, children of divorce internalize things to where they figure that it was *their* bad behavior that somehow triggered the tension between their parents. Let your children know that such feelings are nonsense, without making them feel foolish for expressing them. Tell them that it's a common and natural reaction to feel as if they might have done something to drive their parents apart. Tell them how it gets in kids' heads to where it takes on a life of its own. See if that's how it is with them.

The other essential element is to talk up the benefits of family. *Your* family. Remind your children that no matter what happens, that even though Mom and Dad won't be living together, you will still be a family. Now and forever. Make a family tree if you have to, to illustrate the point. No matter what, the message should be: We will always appear on that family tree as a unit. There is no dividing us. We will stay a family as long as we're on this planet. And here it's not enough to say it—parents have to live up to their words. At family gatherings, set aside your differences and participate together. At life-cycle events, remember your promise to your children. If your ex's father dies, be sure to attend the funeral—and take part in the private, family mourning, too. After all, the man was the grandfather of your children.

In good times and in bad, the children must continue to see you, face-to-face, as civil, communicating adults. If there's anger or door-slamming at the front and back ends of visitation times, the children will take that as slamming the door in *their* faces. Even if it's not totally genuine, make the effort for your children. Make the effort, and succeed at it. And save the venting for another time and place.

Punctuate the process by highlighting for your kids that the intended by-product of the divorce is a happier set of parents. (After all, isn't that the point of the whole deal?) The parents may no longer be together, under the same roof, but if each was driving the other crazy, then it follows that each will become a happier, healthier person in the transformation. Stress that this "recovery" will result in richer, more honest relationships with each parent—and more one-on-one quality time than the child might know what to do with.

Montel: One of the great exercises that Jeff uses in family therapy and divorce mediation is to get divorcing couples to draft and sign a parenting contract that spells out what each expects from the other, and reconfirms their shared commitment to the emotional health of their children. It's not a binding contract—in fact, Jeff has run into some interference from attorneys who don't want such a document muddying up the rest of their divorce paperwork—but it can be a powerful tool.

Keep the lawyers out of it. "This is what we're going to do. This is what we're not going to do." Spell it all out. Any loving parent, when pressed, can find a way to resolve their issues and produce a workable, loving agreement of this kind. Instead of focusing on what you've done wrong and how much you hate each other, keep the focus on your children. What do you want for *them* in the months ahead? What kind of environment do you want them to grow up in? What sort of relationship do you want them to have with your ex?

Do What's Best for the Kids

Visitation, as far as we're concerned, shouldn't even be an issue. More and more, the courts are dealing with cases of joint custody—and this, at least, is a silver lining to the black cloud. Assume joint custody. Make it a given, and reach for it if you can. If circumstances push you in another direction, that's something else, but if there's a way to make joint custody work, then make it work. Why? Well, back when you *had* the kids, you presumably had at least an unspoken agreement to raise those children together, to the best of your shared abilities.

We're not suggesting anything radical here—just that you stick to that basic agreement. Raise your children together. Naturally, one of you will wind up with domicidal custody, and the other with visitation rights, but try to think in terms of what's best for your kids, not what's best for you. But take extra care, if you are the out-of-the-house parent, to ensure that your children are not made to think that you're throwing them out with the spouse. Notice that we didn't use the unfortunate phrase *the out-house parent*, which might accurately describe the shitty role many visitation parents embrace for themselves, or the way some *in-house parents* send signals to their children that this other parent simply isn't useful to them anymore.

In most instances, the out-of-the-house parent will be the father, and it's crucial for the dad to keep fundamentally connected to every aspect of his children's lives. Dads, if you walk away, there's a good chance your kids will wind up in the system in some way, as a negative statistic. Stick around, and keep to a regular visitation schedule that's tighter than once a week. If you're only able to manage weekends, make sure to call as often as possible. Set aside a time that works well for you and for your ex-spouse. And know that, for the first couple of years anyway, your kids will still probably want to talk about the divorce. Over and over and over. Keep the discussion simple, and age-appropriate, but do offer specific answers to specific questions. It's not necessary to talk about your sex life with your ex, but it *is* necessary to respond to the question. If infidelity played a part in the breakup, there's no need to spell this out to your kids—unless of course it's something they're picking up outside the house, in which case you'll want to find a way to express the truth in a manner they can understand.

And if something comes up that you haven't anticipated in your parenting contract, find a way to deal with it. Compromise. If your children ask to see the out-of-the-house parent on an "off" weekend, make it happen. If they want to join a traveling soccer team that requires an every-weekend commitment, help them make that commitment. Remember, it wasn't the children who couldn't find a way to make things work; it was you and your spouse. There's no need to punish them any more than your situation already has.

Live up to whatever bargains you've made with your kids. Don't find yourself a girlfriend in another state, or go looking for that dream job halfway across the country. If these things find *you*, then you'll find a way to deal with them, but try to keep up your end of the deal, and your end of the deal is to hang around. There are a hundred ways to smooth over a disappointment, but no real way to sandpaper those rough spots. We know of one enterprising parent who uses e-mail to keep in constant touch with his child—and while this is a good thing, and far better than no communication at all, it's not nearly enough to make up for the every-other-weekend visitation deal they've got cooking, for the school plays the father is missing, and the bottom-of-the-ninth at-bats he'll never get to see.

Get out of the blame business as quickly as possible. Once the divorce has happened, it's happened. There is no longer blame. Even if your kids never hear you articulating blame, or actually see you pointing a finger, they'll pick up on it if you hold on to it, so let it go. It's over, done. It's time to move on—to a shared future where you can raise your children together with respect, hope, and love.

If you don't respect the relationship you share with your child, then you don't respect the child. Quit those silly, disrespectful games that often accompany divorce, such as fighting and bickering over dollars and cents. The money is pretty much always going to be an issue, at whatever level you are. Goodness, even at the extreme levels, it's an issue. (As we write this, there's a story kicking around the tabloids about a wealthy businessman whose wife is seeking more than $6 million a year in child support. Six million dollars! Not in alimony—child support! As if the *kid* is the one who's become accustomed to a certain profligate lifestyle.) Divide by 10, or 100, or 1000 to find your way back to your own ballpark, and then treat each other decently if you hope to treat your children decently.

Finally, don't hold out any false hopes that things might return to how they were. Family therapists agree that one of the most damaging messages you can send your children in the swirl of divorce is the wishy-washy prospect that maybe the bad stuff will go away and the good stuff will return. For whatever reason, some parents are afraid to close the door on their kids' dreams. Chances are that your children have probably seen any number of those Disney-type, get-the-parents-back-together movies about divorce, and chances are . . . those movies do more harm than good.

You've seen *The Parent Trap,* right? Two identical teenage girls, separated at birth by divorcing parents, conspire to bring those same parents back together to live happily ever after—as a family. It might be wonderful, escapist entertainment, but for children of divorce, especially freshly minted children of divorce, such a mixed message can be enormously destructive. Be sure not to give the impression that your divorce is anything but final. Don't hold out any hope that you or your spouse will ever get back together, because any ounce of hope you might secretly hold for yourself will become a couple hundred pounds of the stuff for your kids.

Don't feed the fantasy. The divorce, and the resulting new living arrangements, should be presented as final. If, by some unexpected twist of fate, you and your spouse decide to get back together at some later point, the news will be greeted as a happy surprise by your kids, and not as an inevitability that it took you a little too long to recognize.

A Working Plan

Robert, 37; and Stella, 35, had decided after ten years of marriage that it was over. Some marriages work, some marriages don't, and this one wasn't working. It happens all the time. They had many friends who'd been divorced, and probably knew more people who were on their second or third marriages than those still working on their first. That was how things were in New York City, in the circles they traveled, and they figured that they'd just deal with it and move on.

But their kids saw things differently. Rob, Jr., age nine; and Cindy, age seven, were each old enough to understand what was going on. They knew the drill; they each had several friends whose parents had been divorced. This wasn't new ground to them on a theoretical level, but it was new ground on a personal level, and they didn't like how it left them feeling. Their parents were constantly bickering. Yelling, even. Sometimes worse. They couldn't walk into a room without feeling the tension, or without one parent trying to play one child off the other. It was hateful and spiteful and downright ugly.

Robert and Stella knew that they were heading down the wrong road, but they couldn't turn things around. They didn't have it in them. They began hearing from their children's teachers. The kids' schoolwork had fallen off, and they were having trouble focusing. Even more distressing, both kids had started to show some behavior problems for the first time in their young lives. They'd all seen divorce—parents and children, both—but it had never looked like this. It was a whole new perspective.

A friend suggested that Robert and Stella try family counseling and divorce mediation in order to save their own sanity, and the sanity of their kids. They showed up in Jeff's office and laid out the situation. It was one that Jeff had seen a hundred times before—and yet he realized that it was raw and new to these good people. It's always raw and new, and no matter how badly people behave, there's almost always some goodness at their core.

Within the first few sessions, it became apparent that

Robert and Stella had fallen into a lot of the negative patterns characterized by couples heading toward divorce. They argued, sometimes violently, in front of the children. They bad-mouthed one another to their kids when they were alone with them. And they couldn't find the time or the patience to lovingly walk their children through what this divorce might look like, and what their lives might look like on the other side.

The couple agreed on a therapy treatment program, which included regular family meetings to discuss a specific game plan, as well as the ramifications of the divorce. They made special efforts to remind the children that they were in no way to blame for the split, and they tried to speak about each other only in respectful terms and tones. As a family, they made a commitment to each other to always remain connected—with Robert and Stella each taking a full share of responsibility as partnering parents. As part of the plan, they also set aside family time for the children to express their emotions, without fear of reprisal. And together they came up with a working model for visitation; they all agreed that Stella would get custody, and that Robert would see the kids every week and call every day.

What they realized as a family in therapy was that they were up against it, and it didn't necessarily take theory to bring them to that point. What they needed was a good shaking, and it seemed that the kids were taking care of that all on their own. Rob, Jr., and Cindy were acting out in what ways they could, as nine- and seven-year-olds, and eventually their parents picked up on their signals. They'd thought divorce would be easy, routine, because that was how all of their friends and acquaintances made it look. People dealt with their issues, rebuilt their lives, and persevered. But it was a different equation when they were in the middle of it. They had no frame of reference. Robert and Stella were angry at each other, but also at themselves, for the way things didn't work out and for putting their kids through such a mess. They didn't have the tools they needed to push forward.

But the kids knew what was what—in their own way. They pointed their parents to the trouble, and they didn't let up until it was resolved. Now they're doing better in school, and they're adjusting to their new lives. Robert and Stella are still not the best of friends, but they're no longer at each other's throats, and they continue to be practical partnering parents to their children.

◆ ◆ ◆

PRACTICAL REGROUPING

L ife goes on, even after a cataclysmic event such as a divorce. Somehow the dog gets fed. Somehow our kids put one foot in front of the other in such a way that they walk through the front door and back into the rest of their lives. Somehow the sun rises and sets, and the roof doesn't fall in. Normalcy—or at least, a routine—returns to family life. There's even an impulse, before too terribly long, to get out there and start circulating again. We're talking about the dreaded "D" word—*dating*—and it rears its complicated head before you know it, which is almost always before you thought you were ready.

Starting to Date Again

We practical parents seem to want to connect with other human animals in the kinds of intimate ways that leave us exposed and vulnerable to all kinds of emotional turmoil—for ourselves, and for our children. It doesn't matter if our hearts have just gone careening on one of those long, loop-di-loop roller-coaster rides into uncertainty. Sometimes the push comes from our kids, or from well-meaning friends and family members, or sometimes it comes from within. Wherever it comes from, it's there soon enough, and we're here to tell you that it's okay to have a romantic life after divorce. For many of us, it's not only okay, it's *essential*. What's not okay, though, is to do so without considering the impact such a move will have on your children, and that's the focus of these next few pages.

Let's get two things straight: There's nothing wrong with dating, and there's everything wrong with parading a long line of "aunts" and "uncles" in front of your children. Do we actually think we're fooling our children with such a charade? We wonder why our teenage boys and girls are so promiscuous at such young ages, and we don't have to look much further than the role-modeling going on in some single-parent households. It's as if the parent expects the children to do as he says, and not as he does. There are kids out there who find someone new at their breakfast tables three or four times a week, or three or four times a month. Goodness, three or four times a *year* is even a little too often to be displaying this kind of behavior in front of your children, in our estimation.

Bringing Someone New into the Equation

First things first. Before the awkward exchange at the breakfast table, you've got to sit your kids down and tell them how it is. Explain to them, if you're out and about and circulating again, that this new person in your life is not meant to replace their mother or their father. This new person is someone you like spending time with, someone who's important to you. You could even offer hope that someday this person might be important to your kids as well, if that's your feeling. Don't inflate the relationship to make it sound like more than it is, and don't undersell it

either. Tell it like it is, as best as you can determine. Set ground
rules, and stick to them.

Jeff: One of Montel's rules for himself, for example, is never
to introduce a new person into his children's lives unless he's
about to embark on a committed, stable relationship. One of the
last things you want, as a newly single parent, is to bring a string
of one-night stands into your home. If it's someone you're only
casually dating, meet elsewhere until it becomes something more
than casual. *Your top priority throughout this period must be your
children.*

Use common sense, and your best judgment. You might enjoy
spending time with this new person, but does this person have a
good enough heart to be around your children in a family setting?
Single moms, a new man coming into your home may be enam-
ored with you, but may not be all that crazy about kids in general, or *your* kids in particular. He might express some initial positive feelings about your kids, but how could this person love your
children the first time they meet? He didn't fall in love with *you*
the first time you met. And one of our big concerns here is not
the obvious concern—that one of these guys will turn out to be a
bad influence on your kids. No, children are exposed to bad influences every day of their lives. The real concern is that your kids
will form an emotional bond with this new person, and then he'll
check out of their lives the week after next. They're already frag-
ile enough as it is as a result of the divorce; there's no need to
make things any tougher on them than you already have.

Also, try to keep in mind that the person you're about to bring
into your home is a stranger in your children's eyes. A stranger,
the boogeyman—whatever you've taught them to be afraid of,
you've now brought into the home. They see that person doing
things to Mom that Dad used to do, touching Mom in ways that
Dad used to touch her. Naturally, it's an upsetting thing, and we
as parents need to be aware of this. We need to avoid it com-

pletely, is what we need to do, but we realize that this is not always possible. We understand that many people have limited means. They can't go out and spring for a hotel room every time they want to be close to someone else. They can't realistically expect to remain celibate until their youngest children are out of the house.

For two single parents, each with kids at home, trying to get together can be a logistical nightmare, so at some point in a new, committed relationship, this issue is going to come up. And when it does, you have to be sensitive to your children's perspective. Sensitive and vigilant and practical. Don't let your date walk around the house in a negligee or pajamas—at least not for a good long while. Don't let your kids have open access to your bedroom. If there are no locks on your door, invest in a simple hook-and-latch down at the hardware store.

And whatever you do, don't throw the whole deal into your children's faces all at once. We can't imagine what kind of unthinking, unfeeling parent would knowingly let kids wake up into such a shocking situation. Go out to dinner, all of you, to get to know each other better. If your date has kids, bring them along. Spend an afternoon or two at the park or the beach. Take in a movie. Move about in conventional, family-oriented ways before you look to spend any private, intimate time together, because even if you think your kids are asleep, even if it's three o'clock in the morning and you're behind two closed doors, and you're really, really quiet . . . your kids will know. They will absolutely know! They'll know and they'll feel left out, which is why it's up to you to *control* what they know so that it doesn't hurt them in any way.

Be honest with your kids. Tell them you're dating. Tell them you're lonely since Dad (or Mom) moved out of the house. Answer their questions. If they ask about sex, don't brush them aside; there's no need to be frank, but they *do* deserve a heartfelt answer, presented in age-appropriate terms. For parents of teenagers, an honest discussion about your own sexuality can be a terrific springboard for a conversation about sexuality in general.

Another thing: Let your children *and* your date know that neither has any kind of authority over the other. This new person will not be allowed to raise a hand to your children, to yell at them, or to discipline them in any way. Be especially clear on this. We don't even think he should be allowed to patiently correct your children's behavior—unless, of course, your kids are smacking him on the butt, at which point it should be okay for this new person to say, "Please don't hit me anymore." But that's it. If your kid makes an inappropriate remark about the weight of your waitress at a restaurant, the reproach should come from *you*, not from your date. If your kid talks too loudly in the movie theater, *you're* the one who should *sssshhhh* him. If your child didn't clean up her room, it's none of this new person's business.

Be especially sensitive to anyone who might manipulate your children in order to win your affections. It happens all the time, and adults who've been away from the dating scene for a while are particularly vulnerable to it. Actually, it's your kids who are particularly vulnerable. Men or women, it doesn't matter . . . folks know that the best way to a single parent's heart is through the children, so those are the notes they hit. Just be sure your children don't become too attached until you're sure about this new person's motives. They've already had to deal with enough separation and loss to last a lifetime. They don't need you and your "friend" piling on some more.

Keep the conversation going with your children at all times. Tell them in specific terms what your intentions are regarding any new relationship. If you're just keeping each other company, find the words to explain this to your kids. If you're hoping it could grow into something long-term, share this, too. If you're planning to invite this new person to go on a short family vacation with you after you've been together for some time, make sure that everyone knows the sleeping arrangements up front—a surprise in this area is not a good thing—no matter whom you're surprising.

And, if you're going to go to the trouble to have these conversations, you've got to listen to what your children are telling you. If they can't find the words to tell you, pick up on their signals. To our thinking, the only practical response to a comment such as, "I don't like the way that lady is always holding your hand," is to . . . stop holding that lady's hand. Period. At least stop holding that lady's hand until your child is comfortable with it. Talk to your new companion, and explain the situation. If she doesn't understand what's at stake, and why this is important, she's probably not a person you need to have in your life. Perhaps you can even suggest to her that she find appropriate ways to reach out to your child, and hold *his* (or her) hand, which in time might lead to the three of you holding hands as you walk down the street. Realize, this is not a time to stand up to your child. This is a time to listen to his concerns, and act on them.

Things change, somewhat, once you cross the threshold into a more stable relationship with this new person. This is someone you want to keep around for the long haul. It's possible that you might even want to remarry, but if you do, now that your kids are involved, and possibly the other person's kids, too, there are a couple things that you need to do first. You need to sit this new person down and make up one of those lists we asked you to make at the beginning of this book. What kind of stepparent do they hope to be? Ask them what they liked about their own parents and what they didn't like. If they're parents already, grill them on some of their values, on some of the decisions they've made along the way. Are they happy with the kind of parent they were before their marriage ended? If there's any kind of thinking that doesn't seem to mesh with your own, this is the time to talk it through. Be especially clear that you don't want this person to take on the role of a surrogate mom or dad. If you're a woman, even if there's no biological father in the picture, a marriage license does not give this new person license to be a parent to your child. That's something that will have to be earned over time—or not.

Jeff: Here again, discipline is out of the question. Montel has had three separate psychologists on three separate segments of his show over the past year, and each one has stated unequivocally that stepparents should have no right to raise a hand to their partner's child. Ever.

As for other kinds of discipline—punishment, scolding, corrective lecturing—these kinds of privileges (and it *is* a privilege to help raise a child) also have to be earned over time. You will need to have a working behavioral contract, especially if your spouse also brings children into this new marriage, because if you don't take the time to delineate each other's role, you'll wind up in an unworkable situation. You'll take the legs out from under your partner. Your kids will play one of you off the other. They'll say things such as, "I don't have to listen to you; you're not my father." And they'll be right.

Once you establish a strong relationship, and a certain level of trust, then obviously some of these caveats go out the window. But until the stepparent is fully accepted as a card-carrying member of your family, it's best to keep all aspects of discipline to the biological parent.

Blending In

In his practice, and on his daily call-in radio show, Jeff counsels numerous families attempting to redefine the parameters of their shared existence. With divorce rates ever-rising, the high incidence of remarriage and repartnering has left the American family looking like a patchwork quilt, with pieces of one family sharing space alongside pieces of another. The old saccharine *Brady Bunch* model has given way to an entirely new dynamic, one that can be as bitter as it can be sweet—and one that rarely works quite so well in fact as it might in theory.

Richard, an accountant, was a 42-year-old widower who had a 16-year-old daughter, Jan. Tammy was a 35-year-old divorced x-ray technician with no children. Together, they would make some classic missteps, and some courageous progress, as they worked to build a new family.

After dating for 14 months, Richard and Tammy decided to get married. There was no trial, living-together period, because Richard worried how it might look in Jan's eyes, and also because Richard and Tammy were clearly committed to one another. However, as it turned out, the issues confronting the new family had little to do with husband and wife.

Tammy, when asked, was outwardly supportive of moving into Richard's home—the same house he and Jan had lived in with Richard's late wife. The territorial issues surrounding that kind of move, in this kind of situation, are often weighted against the new couple; but in this case, those issues weren't the ones on the surface—at least not at first. In fact, for the initial few months, the domestic picture could not have been cheerier. Richard, Tammy, and Jan had all lapsed into an easy, natural routine, and it seemed that this "quilt" would blanket this new family with warmth and caring for a good long time.

Ah, but it was too good to last. Soon enough, as Jan strayed and needed discipline, Tammy found that she had no authority over her husband's child. Jan would shout out, "You're not my mother!" whenever Tammy raised an issue, or attempted to enforce a punishment. "I don't have to listen to you!" Jan would scream. And, indeed, the child was right. She didn't have to listen to Tammy, because Richard and Tammy had never taken the time to spell out the ground rules in this new relationship. They simply assumed that their family would work the way other families worked—that the adults would be in charge and the children would follow. But here, that assumption was complicated by all kinds of issues.

Richard, too, was not entirely supportive of Tammy's efforts at discipline. He didn't know how to put his feelings into words, but he secretly resented it when his new wife punished his daughter. He felt that it was his job, not hers, to be the disciplinarian. The bottom line was that Jan was his child. Tammy was his wife, but not his child's mother. There was, he felt in his bones, a line she could never cross. In their own ways, without ever communicating the thought to each other, Richard and Jan each felt that Tammy was trying to take the place of Jan's mother.

Their home became a battlefield—at first torn over typical teenage issues such as homework and curfews and talking on the telephone, but over time, these difficulties moved onto some important, fundamental territory such as authority and respect. Tammy had come from a background where children were sometimes slapped or spanked, but when she raised a hand to her husband's child, all hell broke loose. It was a disaster area, shot through with resentment and contentiousness.

In family therapy, Richard and Tammy presented a workable game plan for disciplining Jan, and a united front. Jan articulated her feelings that Tammy sort of swept in and took on a parenting role, without first gaining the respect and trust of her stepdaughter, or developing a relationship independent of Richard. Jan was given a chance to vent, and to openly share her concerns about someone like Tammy coming in and "replacing" her mother. She also spoke about how humiliating it was to be spanked, at her age, by a woman she hardly knew; and once these issues were out in the open, the new family appeared to reach a new threshold of understanding.

On the discipline front, Richard and Tammy agreed that they would both have a hand in controlling Jan's behavior, and that each would support the other when punishments were meted out. The one area they couldn't agree on—when to raise a hand to the child—was set aside for Richard to consider. Tammy could withhold privileges (watching TV, telephone and computer time, nights out with friends), but only Richard could administer spankings, or restrain Jan with force if her behavior ever warranted such a response. In this way, it was believed, Tammy wouldn't have to approach that "line" that Richard had drawn in his thinking. And in this way, they could move forward.

What this new family took away from therapy was a willingness to work on whatever it was that needed working on, and an articulated commitment to each other as a family. They were able to retrace their one misstep—racing headlong into remarriage without first considering its many implications or talking them through—and return to sure footing.

◆ ◆ ◆

···CHAPTER···
TWELVE

PRACTICAL PARENTS AND DRUGS

According to a 1998 University of Michigan study on drug use among American youth, our kids are in more trouble than we think. More than 81 percent of high school seniors reported some level of alcohol consumption, 65 percent had smoked or chewed tobacco, and nearly 50 percent had at least experimented with marijuana.

We set these numbers down as a caution for you readers with older children, and a warning about your younger children's future. Our experience tells us that it's never too early to start worrying about the encroachment of drugs and alcohol into the lives of our children—so we worry. The numbers are troubling, and what's most disturbing about this particular survey is that it covers the so-called good kids—the ones who manage to finish school and move forward positively.

In our poorest communities, where the numbers are even more alarming, drug use has become a way of life—a partner to welfare, a friend to the poor, a pull from education, and a bad model for our children. Drugs (and here we'll include alcohol and tobacco in the mix) haunt our neighborhoods and destroy the potential of our children.

The keys to winning the battle against drugs are education (only here we want to stress the parents' education) and a running start. Let's be practical. No amount of in-school drumbeating is gonna turn those numbers around unless kids get the same message at home—and unless that message takes root at the earliest possible age. It is absolutely essential that parents know the physical, social, and psychological effects of drugs on their children. It's not enough that these very same parents may themselves have experimented with these very same substances. They need to know these things from a whole new perspective. And, it's absolutely essential that our children know that their parents will be ever-vigilant on this all-important issue.

Drug Use Is Pervasive Among All Ages

Drug use is no longer limited to teens. Grade-school kids are learning about drugs and experimenting with them at a disturbing rate, at younger and younger ages. In some communities, the age of first experimentation has reached into the single digits! We've seen some studies that suggest that some inner-city kids are smoking their first cigarettes at age six or seven! In the past, drug dealers hung out near schools, but now they've moved *inside*. Some kids view drug use as a way of acting older, which seems a perverted extension of the way kids used to smoke cigarettes to act the part. Music and movies help to sell the notion that drug and alcohol use is somehow cool, and accepted, and if we look objectively at the situation, we'll see that there simply aren't enough counterbalancing images to go around.

So, first things first. Let's know what we're dealing with here. We don't care what *you* were into when you were in school, but understand that things look a little different from an adult perspective, from a *parent's* perspective. It doesn't matter if you could roll the tightest joint on your dorm room floor, or pound back beers with the heartiest frat boy—you'll likely be clueless when it comes to your own kids.

Naturally, the single best evidence you're likely to find, short of the drugs themselves, is the drug paraphernalia that comes with the deal. Eyedrops, matches or lighters, rolling papers, small metal or glass cylinders . . . if there's a head shop in your kid's room, something's going on. The smell of alcohol, tobacco, or drugs on their breath and on their clothing will soon become evident. Chronic use eventually causes the smell of drugs to emanate from the pores of the skin. As far as the particular smell of each drug is concerned, we'll make it easy for you: Anything that carries an odor out of the ordinary should be investigated.

Beyond the unusual smells, there are other physical signs to look for, including watery or bloodshot eyes, dilated pupils, and the kind of poor hygiene that leaves your child in the same clothing for days on end. Frequent nosebleeds could indicate chronic cocaine use, and an overwhelming sense of fatigue and a lack of appetite are sure signs that something's up.

On the behavioral front, you'll want to look out for any unusual or increased manic energy (for example, a child who can't sit still); deteriorating relationships with family and friends; a *new* circle of friends; problems in school; an uncooperative or hostile demeanor; and a sudden loss of interest in lifelong hobbies, sports, or other favorite activities. If your teenage child is an athlete and has had a dramatic muscle gain or increased energy, watch out for steroid use. Also, be aware of any changes in temperament, especially if your child is unable to control his or her temper. This behavior is called "roid rage," and is caused by the testosterone-like effects of steroid use.

A practical warning: The above signs may not be caused by drug use at all, but may be an indication that the child is experiencing emotional problems or conflicts associated with maturational phases. Something else to consider: Drug use among children may sometimes be a self-medication for emotional or physiological problems that they're experiencing. Getting them off illegal drugs and placing them on prescription medications (monitored by a physician), along with psychotherapy, is a step in the right direction.

Steering Your Kids in the Right Direction

Parents usually don't know how to confront their children when they discover a drug problem; it shocks and confuses some, and scares the hell out of others. But there's a lot you can do to help steer your kids back into healthy, drug-free lifestyles. Confront your children in a calm, objective manner, and express your concern and disappointment. Do not initiate the discussion while they're under the influence of drugs or alcohol. They won't listen to what you're saying, and the situation may quickly get out of control. Instead, wait until they're sober. You can choose to have the discussion either one-on-one or within a family meeting. Determine what you can possibly do to help.

Ask your kids if they're using drugs. Assume that they won't cop to it, but nevertheless tell them about the dangers of drug use, and the negative effects on the body and mind—and on the family. Tell them you love and support them. Try to find out how their drug use began or escalated. Ask them if they *want* to stop using drugs. Reassure them that you'll get them help because help is needed and perfectly normal. (Use the cat-climbing-the-tree analogy to sell the point: The cat has no trouble *climbing* the tree, but it's hard as hell to climb down!)

If you're not completely sure whether the drug use is experimental or chronic, don't hesitate to have your kids evaluated by a health professional (physician or psychologist) who's experienced in diagnosing adolescents with alcohol and/or drug-related problems. Ask your family doctor, or call a local medical clinic for recommendations.

Experts have discussed the pros and cons of forcing kids to provide urine or hair samples for drug testing. Many are afraid that the tests will put the children on the defensive and cause a communication breakdown. Our thinking on this one is clear: If they're using drugs, chances are that there's already a communication problem, so testing them is not going to make it much worse. Therefore, if you need tests to get a better idea of the extent of your children's drug use, then do it. However, resort to drug tests with extreme caution, and understand that most kids are resourceful enough to confound the results of the test.

Be consistent and firm in your punishment. Don't be swayed by promises that the drug use will stop. We'll let you in on a little secret: People on drugs lie, lie, and lie. Why? Well, they don't want you to know what's going on, but they're also in denial. They don't see themselves as addicts, but more as recreational users—just hangin' with the homies. To them, it's no big deal; to you, it's everything. Here's where you'll need to deploy some of that "tough love" you've heard so much about. Ask yourself the question: "Do you want to pay now, or pay later?" Better that your kids should get the discipline from you, with their best interests at heart, than from a judge in a court of law, where their best interests often don't enter into the equation.

If you're not making headway in steering your kids away from drugs, then consider sending them to a short-term, in-patient substance abuse center. It's not as extreme as it sounds. Quite often these centers are not only able to get kids off drugs, but they also evaluate and address the behavioral or emotional problems that may be the cause of drug-taking behavior in the first place. At the same time, think about segregating your kids from their drug-using peer group by suggesting that they associate with a different group of friends.

Examine your own behavior, conflicts, and family dynamics to see if there are causal factors (for example, your own smoking and drinking habits) that you can eliminate to make it easier for your kids to recover. Children study and emulate most of your behaviors, both consciously and unconsciously. If you don't believe us, just look at all of your parents' behaviors that you hated but started repeating anyway (and don't try to hide those plaid pants and two-toned shoes—we can *see* them!).

If *you* smoke, if *you* drink more than casually, and/or if *you* take drugs, the chances are greatly increased that your kids may pick up one or all of these habits. You just can't tell your kids not to drink or use drugs if you're saying it with a glass of wine in your hand and a cigarette or joint in your mouth. A good time to mend your ways and give up these bad habits is when you start having children, but if it's too late for that, there's still time to quit. Talk about your struggle to break these negative habits with your teenage children, and make sure that there's nothing two-faced about your condemnation of their behavior.

The practical parent is always on the lookout for a shift in a child's behavior, and it's never too soon to adopt a vigilant stance on drug use. Talk to your kids *before* they start using drugs, when the peer pressures of adolescence begin to surface. A socially aware grade-schooler, in many cases, is not too young to handle such a conversation, especially if it's presented in a thoughtful, constructive tone. Try to be aware of everything that's happening in your children's lives, without being intrusive. Keep the lines of communication open. Establish an open-door policy so that your children will get in the habit of talking to you. Then if you work it right, they'll come to you first with any conflicted feelings on how to handle a particular situation. And whatever you do, don't preach! This is a tough one, we know, but work at it. We parents love to preach—and so do we therapists and talk-show hosts!—but if you want to be heard, you've got to soft-sell your message. Be consistent, and be calm. Be ready to listen. Be quick with praise when your child makes a smart decision.

Know your kids' friends. Know their parents. Visit their homes, and invite them into yours. Make your house a fun place for your kids to hang with their friends after school and on weekends. Invest in a pinball machine or Ping-Pong table, or a big-screen television. And put on the feed! Often, the easiest way to kids' hearts is through their stomach, so be sure to keep an unhealthy supply of the snacks and sodas most kids can't get their hands on in their own homes. Better they should be loading up on sugar and empty carbs under your own roof, then off at someone else's home, unsupervised, ingesting far worse.

Also, consider signing on to any of a number of family wireless plans or paging services to help keep track of your kids, and to help them stay in constant contact with you in the event of an emergency. Keep a list of all your kids' friends' phone numbers, and know where they are at all times. The idea here is not to be suffocating, but to be prudent. If children know they're being monitored, they're less likely to color outside the lines.

If you discover that your kids have friends with drug problems, speak to the parents of those kids and express your concerns. You may have to separate or break up the friendships until the drug problems are addressed. Sit down with your children and explain that they can't be around their drug-using buddies because those kids are emotionally and physically ill. Tell them that as soon as their friends are better, they can hang out again. This is a tough one, we know, but your children may even encourage the drug-using friends to stop taking drugs so their friendships can resume.

Learn what your school district's policies are regarding drug use. Are they invested in zero tolerance? At what grade do they begin teaching drug education? If it's second grade, go them one better and start talking to your child about drugs the year before. Visit your child's school and become part of the policy-making on what kind of drug-abuse education your child will receive. Join school committees that invite outside groups to lecture on the problem.

Know your local politicians, and assertively push for the funding of drug-free activities in your community. Organize local storekeepers or shop owners to clearly ID children who attempt to purchase alcohol or tobacco products. Build a network of like-minded parents, through which any situation out of the ordinary can be easily communicated to other parents and addressed. Sharing experiences about specific approaches to keeping your kids off drugs will be helpful to the other parents, and, at the same time, give *you* some tips, too.

Drugs will always offer mighty temptations to our young people, just as they tempted many of *us* when we were young. Reach for as many resources in your community as you can find to answer your questions, and help your kids either stay away from, or get off, drugs. Some of these resources include local clinics, community organizations, clergymen, Big Brother/Sister programs, PAL (Police Athletic League), and DARE (Drug Awareness Resistance Education).

A crucial part of becoming a smart fighter against drugs is knowing what they look like, how they're used, and their effects on the mind and body. Without this knowledge, you can pack it in before you get started! Your kids will surely try to trick you into thinking that nothing's going on. What follows, then, is a primer on some of the more common substances abused by our teenagers today. We don't set this out as an everything-you-need-to-know glossary, but it should be enough to get you through your first bad patches.

Cannabis

Better known as "herb," "pot," "grass," "weed," "tye," "rope," "tree," "Mary Jane," "dope," and "Ganja," marijuana is the most popular of the illegal substances used by our children. It's cheap, plentiful, and easy to buy. It is usually sold in tiny plastic bags as "treys" ($3), "nickels" ($5), or "dimes" ($10). Pot is smoked either in small pipes, bongs (large water pipes), or as hand-rolled joints made from rolling papers. Popular packaged rolling papers are E-Z Wider, ZIG-ZAG, and Bugler.

Visually, marijuana resembles dry parsley, with bits of stems and seeds mixed in. Stronger forms of pot, such as hashish, resemble brown or black cakes or doughnuts the size of one's palm. Hashish also varies in color from clear to black, and is mixed with tobacco. Pot usually gives a mellow high, which causes a serene, sometimes goofy sense of well-being and euphoria. Despite the claims of health-conscious potheads, marijuana has more cancer-causing agents than tobacco smoke—and, because the unfiltered smoke is usually held in the lungs for as long as possible, marijuana can cause extensive damage to the lungs and pulmonary system with long-term use.

Marijuana has not traditionally been considered as addictive as heroin, but it is just as habit-forming as nicotine and tobacco; worse, it has mind-altering capabilities that can lead to tragic misbehavior, such as driving accidents, spatial miscalculations, or gross errors in judgment.

Cocaine

Also known as "coke," "snow," "blow," "nose candy," and "Lady White," cocaine, which resembles a white crystalline powder, stimulates the central nervous system, causing feelings of excitement and euphoria. Crack cocaine, better know as "crack," comes in a crystalline rock form, is extremely addictive, and its powerful effects can be felt within seconds, although this high is very short-lived.

Cocaine increases the heart and respiratory rate and also causes elevated blood pressure, which can sometimes result in strokes and heart attacks. Continual use can lead to insomnia, loss of appetite, and paranoia. Due to appetite loss, malnutrition can easily occur, which is why many cocaine and crack addicts typically lose weight quickly and look emaciated. The drug can be injected, but it's usually snorted nasally, which eventually damages the mucous membranes and leaves many addicts sniffling as if they have a cold. Crack cocaine is usually smoked in a pipe. These pipes can be made out of anything, including aluminum cans. Crack addicts have short fuses and empty wallets—a dangerous combination.

Other Stimulants

There are various man-made drugs that stimulate the body and mind as much as cocaine. These stimulants are known as amphetamines and meta-amphetamines. They go by such handles as "speed," "uppers," "pep pills," "black beauties," Dexedrine, "crank," and crystalline "Meth." They come in pill and powder form, and can be swallowed, injected, or inhaled.

Inner-city kids, for the most part, tend to avoid these drugs, but parents should note that Ritalin and Cylert are two stimulants that are frequently prescribed for ADHD. Since many inner-city kids have been diagnosed with ADHD and have been put on this medication, there's always the potential for abuse. Indeed, both medications are now being abused in record numbers by the middle-class, suburban youth population (they're being traded for marijuana and cocaine!). So if you have a child with ADHD who has been legitimately prescribed either of these medications, watch out for any possible abuse or recreational use.

Narcotics

Heroin, codeine, morphine, and opium are well-known and widely available narcotics, which are major drugs that cause major problems. Narcotics (from the Greek word for "numbing") produce a feeling of elation that is often followed by nausea, vomiting, and drowsiness. Drowsiness is a symptom characterized by classic head-nodding. A tolerance to these drugs can develop quite rapidly and create a strong dependence. Then, over time, the addict needs more of the drug to get the same high. These drugs can be injected, smoked, inhaled, or taken orally. Heroin is a white or dark brown powder or tarlike substance. Codeine is a dark liquid that can also come in pill form. Morphine can come in white crystals or injectable liquid. Opium can be found in the form of brown chunks, or powder.

Among narcotics, the use of heroin is on the rise, which is also known as "smack," "horse," and "junk." In the past, the favorite way of using heroin was through injection, but in response to the threat of HIV-AIDS transmission through dirty needles, most users have switched to snorting heroin through the nose.

The first use of heroin is trying to tell you something: The first time you snort heroin you get nauseated and throw up. You snort it the second time and it feels great. You snort it the third time and you're hooked.

Trying to detox from heroin is extremely difficult and painful, and most often can only be accomplished in a hospital or an inpatient drug rehabilitation center.

Depressants

Depressants are legal drugs that require a prescription. They include barbiturates, methaqualone, and tranquilizers. Depressants are usually prescribed to relive anxiety and promote relaxation. Their effects are very similar to that of alcohol. However, they've been chronically abused, and in larger doses have caused altered perceptions, slurred speech, depression, and, at worst, coma or even death. Mixing depressants and alcohol, which increases the strength of both of these drugs, has caused many deaths.

Barbiturates have street names such as "downers," "red devils," "blue devils," and "yellow jackets." Methaqualone is better known by the name Quaaludes, or simply "ludes." The best-known tranquilizers are Valium and Librium. All of these drugs are manufactured in pill form.

Depressants quite often are taken to balance out stimulants, so if you suspect that your kids are taking either depressants or stimulants, chances are that they might be taking both.

Hallucinogens

Examples of hallucinogens are PCP (phencyclidine), LSD (lysergic acid diethylamide), mescaline, and psilocybin, all of which can cause both paranoia and hallucinations. PCP is especially unfortunate because it produces wild behavior. Also known as "angel dust" and "lovely," PCP blocks pain receptors in the brain. It also lowers impulse control, causing many kids to go on PCP crazes and get completely out of control—doing damage to others, and, of course, themselves. Continued use of PCP can cause convulsions, coma, and heart and lung failure. PCP comes in powder, liquid, and pill form; and therefore can be taken orally, injected, or sprayed on marijuana joints or cigarettes.

LSD also carries the name "acid," "dots," and "purple haze." It can be taken in tablet form or licked off small pieces of paper. The dots are tiny, but don't be fooled—they're extremely powerful. Mescaline, also known as "mesc," comes in tablet form and can usually be chewed or smoked. Psilocybin, a type of mushroom, is eaten and is sometimes cooked in food. It produces a more powerful high than marijuana and promotes a sense of well-being, but it can cause hallucinations.

"Designer" Drugs

Black-market chemists have modified the molecular structure of some legal drugs to produce so-called designer drugs. Sometimes these drugs are much stronger than the ones they originally copied, but the dosage strength is not visually apparent. That's why there are so many accidental overdoses among young people; they just don't know how lethal these drugs really are. They're so strong that sometimes as little as one dose can cause long-term anxiety, depression, impaired perception, and even brain damage.

The most popular designer drugs are synthetic heroin, "China White," and "ecstasy" (or MDMA, short for methylene-dioxymethamphetamine). All of these drugs provide an initial euphoria and a sense of well-being. However, continued use can cause tremors, impaired speech, and paralysis. All of them usually come in white powder form and are either snorted, inhaled, or injected. These drugs are too powerful to cause an addiction, but are used on special occasions (parties and proms) and provide a euphoric jolt. A recent study indicates that ecstasy can cause long-term genetic impairment and has caused brain damage in animals.

Rohypnol ("Roofies")

Rohypnol is the brand name of a drug called flunitrazepam, on the street better known as "roofies." It is a sedative that is ten times more powerful than Valium and has gained a notorious reputation as the "date rape drug." With no taste or odor, it can be slipped into an alcoholic drink and cause dizziness and disorientation, ultimately causing the victim to pass out for hours without remembering what transpired.

Anabolic Steroids

Steroids were artificially created in the laboratory back in the 1930s to mimic the effects of the male sex hormone testosterone, and they've been used legitimately to treat severe burns and certain types of breast cancer. Steroid use has become a popular illegal drug for athletes. The abuse of steroids has literally been on trial in Germany—six sports officials from the former East Germany were accused of routinely giving 19 of their female Olympic swimmers banned steroids between 1975 and 1989 to make them stronger and faster. Weight lifters and wrestlers are attracted to steroids to quickly increase their muscle mass and definition without the traditional method of extensive workouts.

The major problem with steroid use is the aftereffects. In men, this can cause impotence, sterility, and withered testicles. In women, steroids create masculine traits such as breast reduction and facial hair. Prolonged use of steroids can cause heart attacks, strokes, depression, and sterility. Secondary side effects of steroid use include purple or red spots on the body, swelling of the feet and lower legs, darkening of the skin, unpleasant breath odor, as well as the inability to control one's temper.

With more and more of our children involved in athletics, especially team sports, they may be tempted to use steroids as a shortcut to enhance physical development and ability. If your kids are into sports, stay vigilant about the warning signs of steroid use, but, more important, warn them beforehand. The best sales pitch: *Boys don't want to grow breasts, and girls don't want to grow beards.*

Inhalants

Inhalants include nitrous oxide, amyl nitrate, butyl nitrate, chlorohydrocarbons, and hydrocarbons. Deeply inhaling the vapors of these drugs can cause a quick and joyful high that only lasts a few minutes. However, even short-term use of these drugs can cause nausea, sneezing, coughing, nosebleeds, headaches, and involuntary urination and defecation. Long-term sniffing or inhaling can cause permanent damage to the nervous system.

Nitrous oxide, better known as laughing gas, is sold in small eight-gram metal cylinders with a balloon or pipe propellant. Amyl nitrate, also known as "poppers" or "snappers" (you snap them in half and inhale, especially during sex and before orgasm), is a clear yellowish liquid encased in ampules. Butyl nitrate, better known as "rush," "bullet," and "clima," comes in small bottle cylinders. Chlorohydrocarbons are represented by aerosol sprays or cleaning fluids, and can be found in spray paint cans. The hydrocarbons are actually solvents and can also be present in gasoline, glue, and paint thinner.

Folks, our kids are starting to use inhalants in record numbers. Why? These drugs are cheap, plentiful, easy to purchase, and can easily be found in bathroom and kitchen cabinets. Very small children as young as age five and up are starting to sniff airplane glue and the white creamy glues. So you need to be very careful about keeping solvents and other chemicals in the home.

Alcohol and Tobacco

Alcohol and tobacco are legal drugs that can be as dangerous as any illegal substance if abused. In some ways, they can be more dangerous because they're more socially acceptable, more abundant, and their abuse can be disguised.

— *Alcohol* use over prolonged periods can cause permanent damage to vital organs such as the brain and liver. Pregnant mothers who drink are more apt to give birth to low-weight babies, and, in worst cases, can give birth to babies with fetal alcohol syndrome. Alcohol in young people impairs judgment and lowers inhibitions, both of which can lead to self-destructive behaviors such as violence and physical abuse—as well as to unwanted pregnancies.

The most popular type of alcohol among inner-city adolescents and teens is beer, particularly malt liquor. Beer is bad enough, but malt liquor is worse, having several times the percentage of alcohol compared to regular beer. In some regions, malt liquors have become the companion drug to marijuana.

— *Tobacco*: This substance is responsible for the deaths of more than 100,000 people each year. It is the chief cause of coronary heart disease and lung cancer; and can also lead to cancer of the larynx, esophagus, bladder, pancreas, and kidneys. Smoking cigarettes during pregnancy is risky because smoking mothers are more apt to have spontaneous abortions or preterm births and to produce low-birth-weight babies.

Although the use of chewing tobacco and snuff (powdered tobacco) is rare in the black community, you still need to be on the alert for it. It's commonly sold in cellophane pouches, with a very popular brand being Red Man. The kids usually take a pinch and stuff it between the cheek and gum. Because of the accumulation of the gastric juices, saliva, and tobacco fluids, users must spit often. Many of our kids (and parents) have been fooled into thinking that chewing tobacco is harmless because it's not inhaled. This is the furthest thing from the truth, and another fact that the tobacco companies hide from the public. The risk of cancer from chewing tobacco is just as high as from smoking it. As a matter of fact, cancers of the mouth and other associated areas have continued to rise.

Smoking, in truth, causes bad breath, fuzzy thinking, impotence, lung cancer, and ultimately death. Tell your children that if they want bad breath, bad grades, sex problems, and a slow death, they ought to consider smoking. Sometimes the "negative sales" approach works to discourage bad behavior, so you should try it! Also, ask the school principal to show the video in which a pathologist cuts open the lungs of a dead smoker and compares the tar-ridden organ to that of a nonsmoker.

Herbal Tobacco Substitutes

Trendy herbal substitutes for cigarettes and snuff are now being sold in smoke shops, convenience stores, and, would you believe, even health-food stores. These substitutes are made from blends of herbs, honey-soaked tea leaves, process-flavored lettuce, and flower petals. The more popular brands of herbal cigarettes are Herbal Gold and Honey Rose. The herbal snuffs are Sipstop and Bacc-Off, to name a few. Although it's true that these products are nicotine free, they still have varying amounts of tar. Kids erroneously think that they can't get diseases using these tobacco substitutes, but studies show that health risks still exist from smoking any kind of cigarette. Inhaling smoke, with or without nicotine, is harmful to the human body.

Don't be fooled, parents—herbal tobacco is not good for your children. As one health official put it, "You're supposed to *eat* your vegetables, not smoke them."

The Kids Next Door

Montel has been on the frontlines in the fight against drugs for many years. Long before the launch of his syndicated television show, he traveled the country speaking to kids about staying in school and staying off drugs. And he has repeatedly used his unique television platform to deliver the same message to an even broader audience.

His efforts in this area have not gone unnoticed. Several years ago, Montel was asked by the White House Office of Drug Control Policy to direct a series of public service announcements on the subject, and Montel went looking for real teenage drug addicts to use in the spots. The lockstep impulse, he felt, would have been to hire actors to play these roles, but Montel and his producers wanted the message to really hit a nerve, so he scanned New York-area rehabilitation facilities for the real deal. What he found was a revelation. The teen rehab centers were not populated by stereotypical inner-city kids—the kind Montel might have cast if he had gone about things in another way. For the most part, what he found were clean-cut, middle-class and upper middle-class kids. Kids who didn't look the part. Kids who could have mixed in as comfortably at a country club social as at a rave.

Kids, plain and simple.

One of those kids was a 16-year-old girl named Stacy—a beautiful, blonde-haired, blue-eyed straight-A private-school student from an upper middle-class neighborhood. She'd been drinking and getting high for five years, and it took a near-fatal accident involving one of her friends for her parents to learn the truth—and for Stacy herself to recognize the wrong road she'd embarked on.

No one ever suspected this beautiful, high-achieving little girl of being anything but a beautiful, high-achieving little girl, but she'd been dancing around trouble since she was 11 years old. It started with a couple tastes from her father's beers, and then moved into her father's liquor cabinet. Until she hit 13 or so, Stacy mostly just drank, but once she reached junior high, she started smoking marijuana. Then came the other stuff. She got to where she'd try anything she could get her hands on. She was on something most of the time, and yet she still managed to get good grades. Her teachers never suspected anything, and her parents were also in the dark. Stacy had an older sister who did her share of experimenting, too, but nothing close to what Stacy was doing, and their parents would have sooner suspected the older sister of addiction than Stacy.

Stacy, too, never believed that she had a problem. She thought she could quit anytime she wanted to. She thought she was just having a good time. Everything was under control. She could even get high during school and not miss a beat. She'd ace her exams and participate in class discussions. She was famous among her friends for the way she could move about in a straight world even when she was totally wrecked. And then, one night, something terrifying happened. One of her friends overdosed at a party. It could have been Stacy. They were taking the same stuff, mixing it with the same drinks. It was just dumb luck that she didn't overdose—and dumb luck that the paramedics arrived in time to resuscitate her friend. Trouble was, the *paramedics came with the police, the party was shut down, and all of Stacy's friends were taken down to the precinct house and tested. Stacy's blood-alcohol level was twice the legal limit. She also tested positive for narcotics.*

When Stacy's parents were called and told of the situation, they were shocked. Her parents had been happily married for 20 years, and they thought they were two of the most blessed people in New York. They had good jobs, enough money to live comfortably, and two daughters who had never given them a whiff of trouble. They thought at first that there had been some sort of mistake. They knew these other kids at the party, and they didn't doubt that some of them might have been involved with drugs, but surely Stacy knew better. Surely they *knew Stacy better.*

But there was no mistake. Stacy tearfully admitted her long history of drug and alcohol abuse to her parents, and her mother was so thrown by this turn of events that she had to be helped from the room. Really, it was just about the last thing she was expecting. Interestingly enough, watching her mother react in this way was a wake-up call for Stacy. She loved her parents, and she loved how she looked through their eyes. She wanted them to be proud of her—the way they were when she brought home good grades from school. She hated that she'd disappointed them. She couldn't stomach the thought of how she now looked to them.

With the help of a therapist, Stacy was placed into a rehab facility for a six-month treatment program. She was five months in when Montel met her, and she confided that she was afraid to go home. She was committed to staying sober, but she worried how her transformation would be accepted among her friends. She knew how it would go. She'd have to collect a whole new set of friends in order to stay sober. She prayed that she was up for the challenge.

Her parents had come to visit every weekend and had high hopes. Her sister came, too. The whole family was counting on her, and she was determined not to let them down. All around, there were people telling her she would make it and that they were proud of her, but she was afraid of the social cost of trying. Physically, Stacy had her addictions beat, she felt certain, but this whole-new-set-of-friends business was tough. She liked her friends. They've been with her for her entire life. She was too far along to start over.

"It's like they're a part of me," she told Montel.

"Yeah," Montel replied, "but they're a part of who you were. They're not a part of who you are right now."

◆ ◆ ◆

···CHAPTER···
THIRTEEN

THE PRACTICAL RESPONSE TO TEENAGE REBELLION

There's no place to hide. It turns beautiful children into monsters, changes your house into a war zone, and makes you say terrible things that you always regret later.

And it's coming soon—to a theater near you!

Man, it *does* seem like a horror movie, the way some of our children morph from beautiful little cherubs into headstrong, obnoxious, reckless teenagers, but if you put some of this stuff down in a script, no one would ever believe it—that is, unless they've been through it with their own kids.

Teenage rebellion is the tornado our teens struggle through as they grow from childhood into young adulthood. And, like the call of the wild and other (less romantic) calls of nature, it's inevitable. Most of our kids make it through unscathed, even if most of the parents we know end up with post-traumatic stress syndrome. The key to successfully reaching the other side of this stage in your relationship with your child is to approach it in much the same manner as you've approached every other stage to this point—with intelligence, a positive outlook, and boundless good cheer. Although it's easy to view teenage rebellion as being the problem of the teenager alone, in almost every instance, the family is also very much affected by this turbulent time. Once-peaceful alliances are recast as conflicted and troublesome relationships—and, just like in the harmless horror movies you take in down at the multiplex, you'll quickly find that there's no place to hide.

In the worst-case scenarios, family members lose sight of each other as thinking and feeling people, and start to regard one another as one-dimensional characters consigned to negative roles. The typical family constellation in a "rebellious" household might look something like this: The rebelling teenager becomes the "bad seed," or the "child from hell," while the parents become "the enforcers," or "judge and jury." Younger siblings are the innocent bystanders caught in the crossfire. It doesn't take long, in these new guises, for warm relationships to bubble over past the boiling point. Even the relationships between parents and younger siblings are likely to become fractured as a result of all the tension.

Causes and Remedies

To better understand and troubleshoot this difficult time, let's take a closer look at what causes teen rebellion, and how practical-parenting initiatives can leave you better prepared for what lies ahead. During the teenage years, a child makes the transition from adolescence (the onset of puberty, when sexual maturation begins) to young adulthood—a transition that, in most cases, is anything but smooth. These not-quite-adults confront many new responsibilities and major life decisions, such as whether and where to attend college, how to keep themselves safe in increasingly unsafe situations, and when to ignore the wishes of their parents.

Those first steps toward adulthood are not always carefully chosen. For most kids, freedom means following their own minds, making their own decisions, and thinking and expressing their own thoughts. However, too often a teenagers' "own thoughts" seem to be anything that might rub their parents the wrong way. It means examining and challenging all the rules in order to see what fits, and discarding what doesn't; and it's this simple, statement-driven act of "discarding" that parents often interpret as a challenge to their authority.

Parents tend to become fearful of the situations that accompany their teens' physical, emotional, and sexual maturation, and often respond by becoming overprotective and trying to clip their children's wings. They sometimes fail to recognize that the oppositional attitude they're facing is fueled by hormonal changes, with peer pressure and a general disdain of authority thrown in for good measure. This results in buck-wild behaviors influenced by what must at times appear to be the Malcolm X approach—"by any means necessary." This is where many parents check out, many teenagers shut down, and many families are thrown into the kind of tailspin from which they sometimes never recover. It's also where a second honeymoon to Bellevue Psychiatric starts to sound pretty good.

The practical parent never loses sight of the fact that teenage rebellion is a normal part of growing up. A phase. And it's a phase all families share. Your child is not alone. Your family is not like some contemporary version of the *Addams Family,* or the object of neighbors' stares or the subject of their gossip. They've all been there. No matter the behavior—good, bad, or somewhere in between—our kids are not "bad seeds." They're simply waged in a legitimate struggle between who they've been, and who they might become. In other words, they're just trying to define themselves as individuals, different from their siblings, and especially different from their parents. Our goal should be to keep the rebellious behavior from crashing out of bounds, helping our teens through one of the most difficult times in their lives, and setting aside our own egos and power struggles so that we keep our kids safe and our families whole.

Teens will seek to define themselves as young and independent adults in a variety of ways. Some of these expressions are relatively harmless, while other are clearly more serious; still others cause troubling, long-term effects, possibly reaching far into your children's future. Let's start with the more benign transgressions, such as some of the outrageous fashion statements you will undoubtedly be made to endure. You know that look—the baggy jeans, the designer leather jackets, and brand-name sneakers. Body piercing (ears, noses, eyelids, lips, tongues . . .) will also offer a shocking outlet for expression. For some kids, in some communities, it's like a badge of honor to dress in this way, a code—and yet haven't you noticed that the more upset you get at them for dressing in this way, the happier *they* are? The more holes they'll have poked in their bodies? Clearly, that's one of the reasons they do it. They've reached for a style of clothing and personal expression that's so totally foreign to their parents that it becomes uniquely their own.

A real problem does exist, however, when our kids believe that these styles equate to high status. If they don't have the newest Timberland jacket, Air Jordan sneaker, or some other designer item, they don't think they'll be part of the crowd. As we all know, there are teens who become so desperate that they'll simply steal what they can't afford, and this is where we parents have to step up the watch a little bit and take back some of the control we might have been too quick to relinquish. As much as possible, we want to keep our troubles under our own roof, because once your child breaks the law, it's out of your hands. If it's in your house, it's in your control; if it's out in the street, it's gone.

Our teenagers will also lash out with their tastes in music, and for now, those tastes tend to run toward grunge and heavy metal and rap, depending on the culture of your neighborhood community. Gangsta rap is considered by many parents and social scientists to be the major negative influence on the lives of young

African Americans, for example, but it doesn't have to be that way. Strip the music of its power to shock and excite by bringing it into your home, or onto your car radio. Listen to the words. Ask your kids what they mean, and you might find that their tastes in music undergo another shift. One of the last things rebellious teenagers want is to listen to the same music their parents enjoy.

Another thing they don't want is to be told they're not ready to experiment sexually—especially when their raging hormones are telling them the opposite. Teens believe that they're engaging in mature, adult behavior, even when it's patently inappropriate and potentially self-destructive. Because of AIDS and the increasing incidence of other sexually transmitted diseases, more kids than ever before are starting to consider abstinence, but the majority still look to experiment to one degree or another, often for the wrong reasons, and sometimes with calamitous effects. Make sure your kids know that all that noise about safe sex and birth control you drummed into them earlier in their lives still applies.

And here's another worry: Kids who were once academically strong are now flunking out of school in record numbers, and we can't even begin to guess how many parents we've seen—in Jeff's office and on Montel's show—who reach out to us in desperation because their children are doing poorly in school. For many of these kids, performing poorly in school is their way of rebelling. It's one of the only areas in their worlds they get to control, and too often they use these powers to prompt a negative reaction. Often, there are other factors at work. Subtle, sometimes unspoken pressures from their peers get them thinking that good grades are for losers. Here again, we suggest a firm hand in overseeing a child's schoolwork, and zero tolerance for the kind of fall-off in performance that often accompanies the teenage years.

Since almost all teenagers experience some sort of rebellion, it's important to assess your teenager's degree of risk for self-destructive, dangerous, or antisocial behavior. Know where your kid fits on the spectrum, and you can determine the severity of the situation as well as the type or level of intervention needed.

Mild Rebellion

Teens going through mild rebellion will misbehave in ways that do not cause them to become much of a behavior problem in the home or school. They might stay out past curfew or cut classes on occasion. There is some experimentation with smoking and drinking, but nothing that appears patently abusive. Sexual activity usually begins, although here, too, it will be mostly of the experimentation variety. And, of course, there will be occasional arguments with parents. Funky fashions and outrageous piercings dictate their dressing style. You might recognize your own teenagers in this description, but don't go to sleep on it. Your kids' behavior should still be monitored and addressed before it progresses to the next level.

Moderate Rebellion

At this level, there is a great deal more negative, perhaps even destructive, behavior in the home and at school. House rules are more easily questioned and broken. There is more truancy from school, and grades begin to drop more precipitously. There is usually more frequent negative contact with authority figures and possibly with the law. There is also increased drug and alcohol use—measurably more—as well as a significant amount of anger, which is expressed through aggressive behavior, such as fighting with other teens or membership in gangs.

Severe Rebellion

Here you'll find teenagers who have built a wall between themselves and most adults, including teachers, parents, and any other authority figures. There's almost always gang membership. Quite often these kids carry guns or other weapons—not only for defense, but also for bravado. Many of these teens see a jail term as a badge of honor. Selling or using drugs is also an active part of their lives, and sexual activity becomes reckless.

Somewhere in these thumbnails, you might recognize your child—or, at least, the type of child your teen is about to become. We stress that it's essential for you to be there for your teen, because the struggle and turmoil experienced at this stage of life separates the men from the boys and the women from the girls. Teen rebellion, in every sense, is truly a rite of passage, and you'll need to help your kids navigate their way to the other side. Successfully negotiating these years can strengthen character, and serve your children well into adulthood, which means that your interactions with your kids with respect to these issues should be focused, reductional, supportive, and inspirational.

This is one of those critical times when your teenager is going to need a strong parent *and* a true friend. And you, dear parents, are going to need a lot of help. Which is why we offer our own brand of emotional rescue: *Montel and Jeff's Eight Steps for Constructively Helping Your Teen Rebel.*

Through thousands of therapy sessions, and thousands of interviews with families in crisis, we've developed these strategies to rescue even the most hardened teens whose behavior was buying them first-class tickets to jail. These techniques have brought together families that were being torn apart by conflict, and have patched wounds some folks thought would never heal. As you're reading the following strategies, keep in mind that you must be consistent in your approach. You've got to do this stuff every day, at every opportunity. Also, realize that these strategies work best when parents work as a team. If both parents are living in the house, then work together. If you're separated or divorced, put your other issues aside and come together on this one. Discuss how you can present a united front. And, single parents, you'll have to really redouble your efforts.

And so, without further drumrolling or chest-thumping . . .

Montel and Jeff's Eight Steps for Constructively Helping Your Teen Rebel

1. Choose your battles. We must learn to weed out the small problems from the large, and concede the less important ones. Resist giving criticism on every issue, and save the firm stands for the really big deals. For example, why make a federal case when your kids stay out past curfew, especially if they're only late by 15 minutes? However, if they violate curfew several times in a month and it's becoming a chronic problem, then by all means, they should be called on it. If you choose to make a big deal out of every transgression, there will be no end to the conflicts and arguments, which in turn will lead to more resentment and acting out by your teenagers.

On a piece of paper, list all of your kids' problem behaviors.

They stay out past curfew.

They refuse to do their chores.

They miss a few days of school per month for no reason.

Their rooms look like pigsties, and they refuse to pick up after themselves.

They wear outlandish clothes.

They smoke cigarettes after school with their friends.

Next, prioritize the list from least destructive to most destructive. You might be able to live with the less destructive behaviors on a temporary basis. Usually, they're not causing long-term physical harm and haven't influenced family relationships, scholastic work, and achievement in general. The most destructive behaviors, on the other hand, threaten all aspects of functioning and relationships.

Begin addressing the most destructive and troubling behaviors immediately, and let up on the least dangerous. Once the real problems are identified, there's less emotional clutter, and you can be more focused on addressing your teens' issues. Chances are that once you resolve the more serious behaviors, the least important ones will cease . . . or cease to be important.

2. Initiate real two-way communication with your teens. If you're like many parents facing this type of rebellion for the first time, you're probably thinking, *How can anyone communicate with these kids?* Trust us, it can be done—in fact, it *must* be done—and there are some straightforward ways of doing so. The most effective approach is to interact with them on their turf, in their space. This means hanging out and joining them in some of their favorite pursuits. The goal is to get your teens more comfortable and less uptight in opening up to you. In this more relaxed atmosphere (where *they* have the home-court advantage), you can talk about their daily activities. You can sort through the various conflicts they may be involved in with friends or even authority figures.

Watch music videos together. Play video games with your teens on the Sony Play Station, and discuss play strategies. (At first they'll beat the pants off you, but you should eventually survive to win a point or two.) Go out to a basketball game to see their favorite players or teams. If you can't afford that, watch the game on television; make popcorn or some other favorite snack. No, they can't have a beer! (And you shouldn't either! Set a positive example.) If your daughter's not much into video games or sports, take her to a hot-ticket concert, or go out shopping together for clothes or CDs.

Most important, keep the hot air out of your stomach and the wax out of your ears, and be willing to listen. Quite often, we parents are too busy lecturing to allow kids the room or the time to explain their feelings. We may think we're saying something profound, but all they're hearing is, ". . . blah, blah, blah!"

3. Be a positive role model. During the teenage rebellion years, you'll be challenged to work with your teen with respect to some explosive issues. At times, your patience will be pushed to the limit, especially as communication breaks down during this stage. But as long as you keep your cool and don't lose your temper, you can deal with the crises.

A 1998 *New York Daily News* survey found that more than 70 percent of teenagers consider their parents to be the most influential forces in their lives. This is a good thing to know—but know, too, that as a result, it's incumbent upon you to not only listen and give good advice, but to do so in a calm and rational manner. If you want your teens to use problem-solving skills when dealing with their conflicts, you've got to set an example and do the same. If you "talk the talk," you better "walk the walk."

4. Never make a decision when angry. Some of the most tragic and accidental cases of child abuse occur when a parent is angry and disciplining a child at the same time. Not only does the child become fearful or equally angry, the disciplinary lesson is lost and, even worse, the parent can injure the child. We often misinterpret situations when angry, and blow them out of proportion. Therefore, attempt to address your kids' rebellious behavior in a rational and calm manner. Utilize the following steps to discipline your teens without anger:

- Do whatever it takes to calm down. Count to ten, take a walk, or listen to relaxing music. Just leave it alone for the moment.

- While you're starting to chill, let your kids know that the behavior in question *will* be revisited later in the day.

- Conduct your own investigation of the situation. Interview others who may have been involved. In this way, you'll know what you're talking about.

- If needed, bring in an objective third party as a voice of reason. Your partnering parent, or a close relative or family friend, will usually do fine.

- Seek advice from other parents who have been through similar situations. Their experiences will give you valuable information and suggestions, and let you know that you're not alone.

When finally speaking with your teens, continue to stay calm. State your piece and allow them to state theirs. Establish a forum for discussing issues that may come up in the future. For example, set aside a weekly block of time where you both can address issues that your kids are facing at home, at school, or out and about. Work it right, and you'll probably find that the problems will be discussed and solved before they reach a crisis.

5. Expose your teen to more positive peer groups. We should never underestimate the importance of peer groups in the lives of our children. In many respects, peer groups often contribute and are supportive of teen rebellion. How often do we complain about our kids hanging out with the "wrong crowd"? According to our kids, however, their friends can do no wrong. If you try to separate your kids from their friends, quite often they will embrace them even more. When it comes to separating them from their cronies, you could more easily remove a brain tumor with a dull scalpel! Instead, use the "back-door" approach, by introducing or exposing your kids to a more positive peer group. Then at least they get to make up their own minds about who their new friends or acquaintances will be.

Where do you find these so-called positive peer groups? It's not as hard as you think. Chances are you won't have to look much past your local sports organizations. Positive peers are athletic, they're involved in the arts, and they're often part of civic organizations. The best way to connect your kids to these groups is to have them attend, on a trial basis, after-school activities such as the school newspaper, orchestra, choir, or team sports. Hopefully, one of these activities will spark their interest. If that doesn't happen, the practical parent might offer an incentive: If they attend one of these groups regularly, maybe you'll kick in toward that new mini-disc system they've had their eye on. Or, something. You've got to give a little something to get a little something—and we're not above a little bribery if it will keep our kids safe and sound.

6. Encourage your teens to take on more responsibilities. Our kids have it easy. They rarely have to work for anything, and as a result, many of them lack moral fiber and backbone. In our zeal to give them a better life than we had as children, we end up spoiling them. They, in turn, begin to believe that the world is to be experienced on *their* terms, and they often rebel when they don't get what they want. During their teen years, this type of behavior becomes even more exaggerated and dangerous. A part-time job can be a particularly positive experience that can also relieve boredom, teach skills, provide confidence, increase self-esteem, and build character. Also, earning a wage will keep your kids from entertaining illegal ways to "earn" money.

If your teens don't have a job, then make sure you assign them a moderate number of weekend or daily chores around the house. There's nothing wrong with paying your kids to do the chores (perhaps in the form of an allowance) as long as they really earn the money by doing a good job. Chores have the added benefit of instilling structure and creating self-discipline.

7. Offer lots of positive reinforcement and encouragement. Everything you are, everything you do, is supported by encouragement and reward. Whether it's a promotion for a job well done, or earning enough to keep food on the table, we all need to be rewarded for our behavior. The same goes for our teens. Earlier in this book, we discussed positive reinforcement as a way for younger kids to develop self-esteem, and this is especially true for rebelling teens. Any productive behavior, large or small, should be praised. Don't overdo it—you want to keep your credibility—but pour it on as thick as the situation warrants. When they clean their bedroom, throw out the garbage, mow the lawn, return the videos, do the laundry or dishes, read a novel from the library, go from a C to a B in a class, help a sibling do homework, or attend an after-school activity, be quick with your support. They'll feel better about the extra efforts they've made, and step up their good-deed-doing in hopes of winning more praise at home.

8. Seek psychological or medical help if your kids are out of control. Some rebellious behavior may be the result of an unexplored emotional or physical problem. This may include something as mild as a learning disorder or something as serious as clinical depression. Children with ADHD have trouble focusing, paying attention, and/or sitting still, among other symptoms, all of which can be misinterpreted as willful bad behavior. In addition, because teens usually can't control these symptoms without therapeutic intervention, they're made to believe that they're misbehaving, disruptive individuals. Proper diagnosis by a health professional, and timely intervention, will not only improve the problem, but also save you and your teenagers a lot of frustration and conflict if you know what battle you're really fighting.

Keep in mind that some behaviors, such as drug-dependent ones, may be partly genetic. If you have a family history of dependency, then your teenager may also be at risk. Seek early intervention at the first sign of trouble.

◆ ◆ ◆ ◆ ◆

Take these eight steps with your kids. Things might get worse before they get better. But keep at it. You'll definitely lose some of the battles, but you'll be much more likely to win the war.

Don't expect changes overnight, but work to maintain constant, steady communication with your teens. Keep your eyes on the prize—a safe, successful navigation of these troubling waters—and you'll start to see results.

Out of Control

Melissa was only 14 when she appeared on the Montel *show. She was already using drugs, and had multiple sex partners. Her mother, Joyce, was afraid that her daughter was going to overdose, or contract a sexually transmitted disease from one of the guys she was sleeping with. She was also crestfallen over the fact that Melissa had appeared in an amateur porn film.*

Joyce felt that she had no authority over Melissa and that she had failed miserably as a parent. Melissa saw things another way—her own way. She felt that her behavior fell under the category of "acceptable teenage behavior." Everyone was doing it, she justified. She was no different from her friends. Kids are supposed to behave in this way. They need to get this stuff out of their system.

This "stuff," to Melissa, included taking acid and ecstasy, marijuana and zanac bars, and drinking alcohol. She said the porn movie she made with her boyfriend was "fun." She defended her sexual behavior by stating that she used birth control. She was failing in school and didn't seem to care. At the time of the taping, Melissa was talking about becoming a stripper. She said she thought that a stripper's lifestyle was glamorous, and figured that since guys were always hitting on her anyway, she might as well make some money off of it.

"I'm so confused and hurt that I'm almost numb," Joyce confided to Montel during the taping. "I go through my daily routine without any emotion. My daughter doesn't

listen to a thing I say. She has no respect for me or her father. She's just a little sexpot."

Well, as it turned out, this little sexpot wasn't as tough on Montel's stage as she apparently was at home with her parents. After some tough questions, Montel's relentless, in-your-face approach eventually wore the girl down. She admitted that, despite her bluster to the contrary, it does matter to her what people think of her. It does matter what her parents think of her. This kind of admission, from a rebellious teenager like Melissa, is half the battle.

Before the taping was through, Melissa and Joyce reached an understanding, of a kind. Joyce agreed to listen to her daughter when she came to her with a problem. Joyce acknowledged that she was very young when she gave birth to Melissa, and perhaps she had not been as attentive as she might have been. Melissa remembered feeling alone and neglected as a young girl, and guessed that perhaps she acted out to get attention. Negative attention was better than no attention, she said.

Obviously, there was no guarantee that Joyce could help Melissa set right the pendulum in her young life, but they were able to make an important start. The two were able to admit to each other that they weren't happy with the direction their lives had taken in general, and with Melissa's out-of-control behavior in particular.

The first step is always the hardest one to take, and Joyce and Melissa took an important first step together that afternoon.

◆ ◆ ◆

···CHAPTER···
FOURTEEN

A Practical Perspective

You know what's funny? One of the best growth experiences either one of us has ever had as parents was getting together over this book, kicking things around, and thinking them through. We highly recommend the effort we've made on this project. It's not up to us to recommend the *result* of that effort (the book you now hold in your hands), but the process has been enormously gratifying. To put a finer point on it, then, it's the *process* we recommend. Which takes us to one last piece of impractical advice: If you ever find yourself at a loss on some parenting point or other, find a good and trusted friend and convince him to write a book with you about it. In the writing, you'll discover what you're looking for.

That's how it's been for us. We thought we knew it all, but when it came time to put it down on paper, we realized we didn't know the first thing. (Okay, so maybe we knew the *first* thing, but we got tripped up on the second and third.) In our day jobs, we'd each collected thousands of stories from families in crisis and parents at pressure points, which combined with our own experiences to form a living, breathing mass of practical-parenting insights. It's just that, until now, we've tended to think of each family we've counseled as a case in point, instead of in context. It's nice to see it all solidified at the back end of this book project—nice to put down labels and concepts and ideas that have been bouncing around in our heads all these years.

More than that, it's nice to have had the chance to bounce these ideas off each other, and see what they look like on the rebound. In the months spent writing, we've learned that even well-known family therapists and TV talk-show hosts can sometimes be two-faced hypocrites, as it was pointed out to us that we don't always practice what we preach. We try, we get close to it, but at some point we invariably drop one ball or another. We're human. But writing this book has kept us honest—and accountable—and having written it together will keep us honest and accountable in the future.

What we've asked of you, we've asked of ourselves. We looked in the mirror and assessed our personal baggage. We pushed each other on some of the tough questions we pushed *you* to consider. We disagreed with each other on some issues.

Jeff: Montel can't wait to see the hate mail I get from stroller manufacturers for my Just Say No stand on four-wheelers! And he couldn't see how anyone would possibly disagree with us on other issues, even though we're confident that someone will. And we reached back over some of the trouble spots we might have mishandled in our parenting lives and tried to make repairs.

What we've accomplished, we believe, holds as true for us as it does for our readers. We've reconsidered what it means to be a parent—what it means on a cultural level, and what it means on a personal level. We've redefined, a little bit, the way we look back at ourselves in the mirror.

Montel: Used to be, when pressed to offer a thumbnail self-description, Jeff might have referred to himself as a psychologist, or a family therapist, or a radio personality.

Jeff: Montel, at various points, was a Naval officer, a motivational speaker, a TV talk-show host, an author, and even an actor. Early on in our marriages, it's possible that we thought of ourselves primarily as husbands. But these days, and forevermore, we think of ourselves as parents. We're fathers first, and if we get time for anything else, we'll try to slot it in.

Does it get any easier, as our kids get older? We can't say for sure. It gets different. The stakes change from one day to the next; the issues morph. Collectively, our six kids now range from the ages of 5 through 16, so we pretty much cover the waterfront on virtually all stages of parenting a minor child. The challenge, we think, is to keep it hard, because when something is difficult to master, you keep at it. You press on. You constantly fine-tune your skills because there's always something you can do better. A conversation you can pursue more gently. A hug you can offer more quickly. A firm response you could have made a little more firm. Parenting should be hard—as the cliché goes, it's the hardest job you'll ever have—and as parents, we should embrace its many-headed difficulties and learn from them. When it gets easy, it means we're doing something wrong.

Do we lose more sleep over the younger ones than the older ones? Frankly, we lose sleep over them all. It's whatever moves to the front of the line that demands your attention at just that moment.

Jeff: During the writing of this book, the front-and-center concern for Montel was the ordeal facing his 11-year-old daughter, Maressa, who was having a congenital birth defect corrected on her right arm, which was nine centimeters shorter than her left. It was a planned procedure, something they had talked about all of Maressa's life, but now that they were in its middle, it was raw, and immediate, and like nothing they expected. After a grueling operation, the child was left with four screws sticking through the bone of her arm, attached to a high-tech device that Maressa herself had to turn each day for a year to stretch her bone. An entire year!

So, yeah, Montel's losing sleep over the physical pain that his daughter Maressa is in, and he's losing sleep over the emotional pain she's in, neither of which she can control. He's worried about what kind of teasing she'll face, with this contraption on her arm, once she returns to school. And he's worrying whether she'll be able to move about with pride in public places—if the ordeal won't claim a piece of *her* even as it adds nine centimeters to her right arm.

For Montel, now, it's been Maressa's turn. Soon enough it will be Ashley's, as she struggles to carve an independent path without lashing out against her parents, or hurting herself. Or Montel II's and Wynter-Grace's, as they recast their family dynamic in the midst of their parents' divorce.

Montel: For Jeff, his kids, Puma-Xavier and Q'vanaa Elektraa, seem to go through the same hoops at roughly the same time, and the issues have lately been finding new and creative ways to help them solve some of the little-kid dilemmas that loom large in their lives. How to reach for independence. How to claim responsibility. How to take care of each other. Also, as a father, how to find time to just *be* with his family—without stressing over work, or fussing with the house, or second-guessing some missed opportunity. His fantasy is to keep at it, to keep cranking out kids until he's too old and too slow to keep up with them. He'd like to be 60 and carrying babies—oops, the secret's out!—because by then he feels certain he'll have found a way to shut off those professional valves and just chill. To just *be* with his kids.

Our plan, as friends and collaborators, is to go at this mountain again—because there's just no way we can touch all the bases on this one pass. We can cover the broad themes, but there are whole books waiting to be written on rebellious teenagers, on pre-parenting techniques, on education . . . and we mean to put our heads together and start writing them. Once we're through with one, we'll probably start on another, because this parenting business is a never-ending thing. There's no finish line to it, not that we can see.

It doesn't matter if they up and move out of the house and make a comfortable place for themselves on their own—your kids are still with you. They're a part of you, always, and there are always new things to learn and explore as those parts of you learn and explore for themselves.

What changes, we guess, are the terms of the parent-child relationship. There's no changing the biology of the thing—or, in the case of adoptive or stepparents, the legal and formative bond. No, it's the contract between parent and child that's up for grabs, and the bottom line is that at some time it's up to the kids to let you stay on the job. When they're at home, under your roof, they're all yours; but when they're out on their own, they get to keep you in their life—or not. They can recast you as a friend— or not. It goes from being your ball to their ball, but if you play it right in those early years, if you follow some of the advice we've offered in these pages and a lot of what's in your heart, you'll get to keep playing for a lifetime.

Let us know how it goes.

◆ ◆ ◆

APPENDIX

A GENERAL READING LIST FOR PARENTS

(approved by the Partnership for a Drug-Free America
www.drugfreeamerica.org)

● ●

Buzzed: The Straight Facts about the Most Used and Abused Drugs, from Alcohol to Ecstasy, by Cynthia Kuhn, Ph.D., et al., 1998. W. W. Norton and Company. $14.95.

*The Fact Is . . . Hispanic Parents Can Help Their Children Avoid Alcohol and Other Drug Problems,*1989. National Clearinghouse for Alcohol and Drug Information, P.O. Box 2345, Rockville, MD 20852. Free.

The Fact Is . . . You Can Prevent Alcohol and Other Drug Problems Among Elementary School Children, 1988. National Clearinghouse for Alcohol and Drug Information. P.O. Box 2345, Rockville, MD 20852. Free.

The Fact Is . . . You Can Prevent Alcohol and Other Drug Use Among Secondary School Students, 1989. National Clearinghouse for Alcohol and Drug Information, P.O. Box 2345, Rockville, MD 29852. Free.

A Parent's Guide to Prevention: Growing Up Drug Free. U.S. Department of Education, National Clearinghouse for Alcohol and Drug Information, P.O. Box 2345, Rockville, MD 20852 (800) 624-0100.

Preparing for the Drug-Free Years: A Family Activity Book, by J. David Hawkins, et al., 1988. Developmental Research and Programs, Box 85746, Seattle, WA 98145. $10.95.

Teaming Up for Drug Prevention with America's Young Athletes. Drug Enforcement Administration, Demand Reduction Section, 1405 I St., NW, Washington, DC 20537. Free.

Ten Steps to Help Your Child Say "No": A Parent's Guide, 1986. National Clearinghouse for Alcohol and Drug Information, P.O. Box 2345, Rockville, MD 20852. Free.

What Every Parent Can Do about Teenage Alcohol and Drug Abuse: Hope and Help from Parents Who Have Been There. Parents and Adolescents Recovering Together Successfully (PARTS), 12815 Stebick Court, San Diego, CA 92130 (800) 420-7278. $9.95 (money-back guarantee).

What Works: Schools Without Drugs. 1986, revised in 1989. U.S. Department of Education, National Clearinghouse for Alcohol and Drug Information, P.O. Box 2345, Rockville, MD 20852. Free.

Young Children and Drugs: What Parents Can Do. 1987. The Wisconsin Clearing House, 1594 E. Washington Ave., Madison, WI 53704. $6.00 for 100 brochures.

◆ ◆ ◆

Family-Oriented Social Service Organizations

African-American Family Services
2616 Nicollet Ave.
Minneapolis, MN 55408
(612) 871-7878

Al-Anon Family Group Headquarters, Inc.
1600 Corporate Landing Pkwy.
Virginia Beach, VA 23454
(757) 563-1600 (US)
(613) 722-1830 (Canada)

Alcoholics Anonymous World Services
475 Riverside Dr.
New York, NY 10115
(212) 870-3400

American Council for Drug Education
164 W. 74th St.
New York, NY 10023
(800) 488-DRUG

American Health Foundation
320 East 43rd St.
New York, NY 10017
(212) 687-2339

Boys and Girls Clubs of America
1230 W. Peachtree St., NW
Atlanta, GA 30309
(404) 815-5700

Camp Fire, Inc.
4601 Madison Ave.
Kansas City, MO 64112
(816) 756-1950

CDC National Aids Clearinghouse
P.O. Box 6003
Rockville, MD 20849
(800) 458-5231

Center for Science in the Public Interest
1875 Connecticut Ave., NW, Ste. 300
Washington, DC 20009
(202) 332-9110

Center for Substance Abuse Prevention (CSAP)
Substance Abuse and Mental Health Services Administration
5600 Fishers Lane, Rm. 800
Rockville, MD 20857
(301) 443-0373
(800) 729-6686 (national clearinghouse)

Center for Substance Abuse Treatment (CSAT)
5600 Fishers Lane, Rm. 618
Rockville, MD 20857
(301) 443-5052

Clearinghouse for Family Violence Information
P.O. Box 1182
Washington, DC 20013
(800) 394-3366

Community Anti-Drug Coalitions of America (CADCA)
901 N. Pitt St., Ste. 300
Alexandria, VA 22314
(703) 706-0560
(800) 54-CADCA

Drug Strategies
2445 M. St., NW, Ste. 480
Washington, DC 20037
(202) 663-6090

Families Anonymous
P.O. Box 3475
Culver City, CA 90231
(800) 736-9805

Girls Incorporated
30 East 33rd St., 7th Floor
New York, NY 10016
(317) 634-7546
(800) 374-4475

Hazelden Foundation
Box 11
Center City, MN 55012
(800) 328-9000

Join Together
441 Stuart St., 6th Floor
Boston, MA 02116
(617) 437-1500

"Just Say No" International
1777 N. California Blvd., Ste. 210
Walnut Creek, CA 94596
(510) 939-6666
(800) 258-2766

Mothers Against Drunk Driving (MADD)
511 E. John Carpenter Fwy., Ste. 700
Irvington, TX 75062
(214) 744-6233
(800) GET-MADD

Nar-Anon Family Groups
P.O. Box 2562
Palos Verdes Peninsula, CA 90274
(213) 547-5800

Narcotics Anonymous
11426 Rockville Pike, Ste. 100
Rockville, MD 20852
(301) 468-0985

National Association for Children of Alcoholics
11426 Rockville Pike, Ste. 100
Seattle, WA 98144
(206) 324-9360
(800) 322-5601

National Association for Native American Children of Alcoholics
611 12th Ave. South, Ste. 200
Rockville, MD 20852
(301) 468-0985

National Black Child Development Institute
463 Rhode Island Ave., NW
Washington, DC 20005
(202) 387-1281
(800) 556-2234

National Center for Tobacco-Free Kids
1707 L St., NW, Ste. 800
Washington, DC 20036
(800) 284-KIDS

National Clearinghouse for Alcohol and Drug Information
P.O. Box 2345
Rockville, MD 20847
(800) Say-NOTO

National Council on Alcoholism and Drug Dependence, Inc.
12 West 21st St., 7th Floor
New York, NY 10017
(212) 206-6770
(800) NCA-CALL

National Crime Prevention Council
1700 K St., NW, 2nd Floor
Washington, DC 20006
(202) 466-6272
(800) 627-2911 (information requests)

National Domestic Violence Hotline
(800) 799-7233
Treatment facility referrals and helpline
(800) HELP-111
General reading list for parents

National Families in Action

2296 Henderson Mill Rd., Ste. 300
Atlanta, GA 30345
(770) 934-6364

National Family Partnership

9220 S.W. Barbur Blvd., Nos. 119-284
Portland, OR 97219
(503) 244-5506 (fax)

National Head Start Association

201 N. Union St., Ste. 320
Alexandria, VA 22314
(703) 739-0875

National Inhalant Prevention Coalition

1201 W. 6th St., Ste. C-200
Austin, TX 78703
(800) 269-4237

National Institute on Drug Abuse (NIDA)

5600 Fishers Lane, Rm. 10A03
Rockville, MD 20857
(301) 443-4577

National Urban League Substance Abuse Program

500 East 62nd St.
New York, NY 10021
(212) 310-9000

Office of Minority Health Resource Center

P.O. Box 37337
Washington, DC 20013
(800) 444-6472

Office of National Drug Control Policy (ONDCP)
P.O. Box 6000
Rockville, MD 20849
(800) 666-3332

Parents' Resource Institute for Drug Education
50 Hurt Plaza, Ste. 210
Atlanta, GA 30303
(404) 577-4500
(800) 853-7867

Safe and Drug-Free Schools Program
U.S. Department of Education
1250 Maryland Ave., SW
Washington, DC 20024
(800) 624-0100

Students Against Drunk Driving
200 Pleasant St.
Marlboro, MA 01752
(508) 481-3568

Toughlove
P.O. Box 1069
Doylestown, PA 18901
(215) 348-7090
(800) 333-1069
www.toughlove.org

◆ ◆ ◆

About the Authors

Montel Williams is the Emmy Award–winning host of the nationally syndicated *Montel* show. As a highly decorated former Naval intelligence officer, motivational speaker, actor, and humanitarian, Williams is an example of personal achievement for people throughout the country. He is the author of the *New York Times* bestseller *Mountain, Get Out of My Way;* an inspirational book called *Life Lessons and Reflections;* and the proud father of four children.

Jeffrey Gardère, Ph.D., a practicing clinical psychologist, has appeared on nearly every major talk and news show on radio and television. He currently hosts *Hit It,* a relationship advice show on WLIB radio in New York. "Dr. Jeff," as he is called by fans and patients alike, is the founder and CEO of Rainbow Psychological Clinics, a culturally sensitive program providing psychological health care for children, adults, and families in the New York tri-state area. Dr. Jeff is the author of *Smart Parenting for African-Americans,* and is a married father of two children, ages five and seven.

◆ ◆ ◆

♦ ♦ ♦

We hope you enjoyed this Mountain Movers Press/
Hay House book. If you would like additional information
about Mountain Movers Press, please contact:

c/o Hay House, Inc.
P.O. Box 5100
Carlsbad, CA 92018-5100

(760) 431-7695 or **(800) 654-5126**
(760) 431-6948 (fax) or **(800) 650-5115 (fax)**

Please visit the Hay House Website at: **hayhouse.com**

♦ ♦ ♦